ISBN 978-1-333-40583-0
PIBN 10500484

# 1 MONTH OF
# FREE
# READING

at

## www.ForgottenBooks.com

By purchasing this book you are eligible for one month membership to ForgottenBooks.com, giving you unlimited access to our entire collection of over 700,000 titles via our web site and mobile apps.

To claim your free month visit:

www.forgottenbooks.com/free500484

English
Français
Deutsche
Italiano
Español
Português

# www.forgottenbooks.com

**Mythology** Photography **Fiction**
Fishing Christianity **Art** Cooking
Essays Buddhism Freemasonry
Medicine **Biology** Music **Ancient
Egypt** Evolution Carpentry Physics
Dance Geology **Mathematics** Fitness
Shakespeare **Folklore** Yoga Marketing
**Confidence** Immortality Biographies
Poetry **Psychology** Witchcraft
Electronics Chemistry History **Law**
Accounting **Philosophy** Anthropology
Alchemy Drama Quantum Mechanics
Atheism Sexual Health **Ancient History**
**Entrepreneurship** Languages Sport
Paleontology Needlework Islam
**Metaphysics** Investment Archaeology
Parenting Statistics Criminology
**Motivational**

# MEMOIRS

## AND

# ADDRESSES

—

### OF

## L. B. McFARLAND

# TABLE OF CONTENTS.

## ILLUSTRATIONS.

# MEMOIRS.    1236219

The collection and publication of the following writings of mine were not prompted entirely by opinion of their literary merits or worthiness of longer perpetuation; or for sale or for general distribution, but for my immediate family, my kin of the McFarland and Douglass clans, of which I am now the oldest, and for a few dear friends all of whom I feel will receive with appreciation and judge without criticism.

In more than one address to my comrades—surviving Confederate Veterans—I urged that they should each write the story of their service to their country, as the best heritage they could leave to their families. Carlyle says, "History is the essence of memorable biography." I, myself, served four years of my youth in the Confederate Army, and I felt that I should not "reck my own read as some ungracious pastors do," and leave undone duties I had preached to my comrades.

Another prompting was that I desired to put in some more enduring form something of the life of my dear father and mother, with tribute to their virtues and worth, and mention of others, friends and families, who have made life sweet to me.

I should confess, however, that beneath these promptings there was that human shrinking from passing to the forgotten; from leaving no evidence of having ever existed. Shelley says, "it is natural to war against oblivion." Losing too, that chiefest reward of human effort and ambition— Remembrance! From the dread of sinking to nothingness and the hope of further life for our name and works spring ambition, toil and the practice of all the virtues. Without the hope of this,

"What youth viewing his progress through
What perils past, what crosses to endure
Would shut the book and sit him down and die."

I was born April 7, 1843, at Dancyville, Haywood County, or Somerville, Fayette County, Tennessee, I do not remember which, as I was then quite young and there has been no contention since between the two places claiming the honor of my birth. Limitation of residence has given me to Haywood.

My parents were Dr. William Felix McFarland and Martha Anna Douglass.

My father was born and resided in Smith County, Tennessee, near the Tennessee River, son of Lewis McFarland, and educated at country schools and at Chapel Hill. He taught school for several years, and then studied medicine at Louisville Medical College, and after securing his diploma settled at Dancyville, Haywood County, Tenn., in 1841.

At the time of his settlement there the country was sparsely settled and a physician's profession and duties were exceedingly onerous. He soon became the leading physician of South Hatchie, his practice extending over some twenty miles of horseback travel, tradition telling of the splendid horses he rode, and his sleeping on horseback on his nightly visits.

His practice enabled him to accumulate a good landed estate and the two enabled his family to live well, and to enjoy a liberal hospitality, as was habitual to the South.

In 1860, he opposed secession vigorously until his state seceded on second ballot, when he became an ardent and active supporter of the Southern cause, so ready, and active in entertaining Southern soldiers, and in guiding Forrests Cavalry in their raids through West Tennessee, that he spent much of his time in the noted Irving Block, Memphis, and gave his only son, then old enough, to the Southern cause.

At the conclusion of the war he was called to Memphis as one of the Professors of the Memphis Medical College where he served for some time. However, he was called so often back to Haywood to minister to his life-long patients, and missed so keenly his old surroundings, and the companionship of his old friends, he returned to the old homestead where he died on Jan. 3, 1878, and was buried in the cemetery there.

DR. WILLIAM FELIX McFARLAND.

His character is well portrayed in a poem by Dr. Bruns, "The Country Doctor" from which these lines are quoted:

"The well beloved of all his peers
But by the poor deemed half divine.

The good old doctor, mild as wise,
With pleasant jest for all he met
The kindly humor in his eyes
Flashed through the lips so gravely sweet.

Firm hand, big heart, and ample brain
Toughened by battles fought and won
Scarred by the wind and winter rain
And bronzed by many a summer sun."

My mother was the daughter of Honorable Burchett Douglass, who lived in Somerville, Fayette County, Tennessee, at date of her marriage, was President of the Bank there and owned a large plantation on Muddy Creek, north of Somerville.

She was a beautiful woman in youth, a comely matron and, a splendid housekeeper in her home; liberal in hospitality, delighting in entertaining her friends, especially during the Methodist Quarterly Meetings, when the house was open to all.

She was a dutiful wife, and affectionate mother. She sent her son to the Southern Army with tearful farewell and the Spartan injunction, and always before his leaving home, kneeling with him in prayer for his safe return; and this son, engaged in many battles felt the more secure from hurt from these prayers. She, however, was the heroine and sufferer of our family. Left alone at home much of the four years of the war with the younger children, separated by distance and the Federal lines, from her son. Communication severed, and daily rumors of battles; and at one period her husband a prisoner at Memphis in the Irving Block, she buried three young children in so many weeks, then brushing the tears of sorrow from her cheeks, she journeyed through snow and sleet in an open buggy the fifty miles to Memphis, with only a boy as companion, to be near her husband, imprisoned in Irving Block. No wonder she died at the early age of forty-five.

Aside from the stirring events of the war,—there was nothing specially romantic or out of the usual in my life.

My education was first at home schools, and then in 1860, I entered LaGrange College, then at Florence, Alabama, founded by Bishop Robert Paine of the Southern Methodist Church, with Dr. R. H. Rivers then President. In the spring of 1861, during my first session there the Civil War came on and soon in its ravages the law became silent, and the halls of learning vacated. I remember vividly the scenes of excitement in Florence the night news of Sumpter's surrender came. The town was wild, bonfires blazed on every street. The students volunteers paraded, and tossed ready caps in air, and made the welkin ring with shouts of rejoicing. My state had not seceded, and had in fact at this date voted against secession, and my people were still for union. I could not join any military company, or participate in the rejoicings in victory. In fact witnessed the scenes that night with feeling of intense sorrow. I remember an incident of this rejoicing,—one of my college class, Clarke of Tupelo, Mississippi, came shouting by me and exclaimed, "Take off your hat and join us." I said, "Clarke, if you will first drape your town in mourning for this war, then so soon as my state secedes I will join in all rejoicing over any Southern victory, though I dread the future."

My state did soon secede. I left college, went home and joined a company then organizing.

When Bragg's army was retiring from Kentucky after Richmond and Perryville, one hot day I was riding past a Mississippi regiment, when I was halted by this same brother student, Clarke, whom I had not seen for months, hot and tired and dirty, and after the first greeting he said, "Mc, I remember that Sumpter night at Florence and what you said; you were right."

Having enlisted our company rendezvoused at Jackson, Tennessee, and became Company "A" of the 9th Tenn., Infantry. We were ordered to Union City, Tenn., and our regiment there became one of a brigade under Gen. B. F. Cheatham, and then for the balance of the war, with temporary intervals of other commanders, in Cheatham's division, and ours and Cleburn's were "brothers in honor" of that army. I was first elected first Corporal of my company, then made Sergeant Major of my regiment at Shiloh, and served as such until April 6, 1863, when I was elected Lieutenant of my company, and there being then a complement of officers in my company by reason of consolidation of the 6th with the 9th Tennessee Regiment. Gen. Geo. Maney then commanding our brigade took me on his staff as Aid, and I served with him up to the evacuation of Atlanta. However, when the army reached Atlanta, the Colonel of my regiment, Col. Jno. W. Buford was made commander of the Post of Atlanta, and he asked for my detail as Adjutant of the Post, and I filled this position until its evacuation, returning temporarily to Gen. Maney's Staff at his request, and participated with him in the battle of 22nd July, 1864, the day Federal Gen. McPherson was killed.

During the siege of Atlanta I witnessed many scenes of suffering, hardship and danger, with courageous endurance of the citizens. I note one incident: Our headquarters were on Peach Tree Street—opposite was a cottage occupied by a widow and two grown daughters, one morning I heard a shell pass over our office, then a crash into this cottage, and screams of women. I rushed over to find the mother and one of the daughters standing in one of the rooms, a chair and the mother's dress torn to pieces, a large hole in the wall and a shell lying unexploded on the floor. It had come through the wall, and through the mother's clothing tearing the chair to pieces on which she was sitting, but fortunately did not explode, nor wound the mother. This woman still remained in this home until the city was evacuated.

Another incident:—The day we evacuated the city there was on the tracks of the railroad a train of cars of considerable number loaded with ammunition of every sort, powder, shell, cartridges etc.  I was directed to burn these cars when sun set.  I took a detail of men, had them place kindling under each car with direction to be ready with burning faggots and on signal given to fire the car and then run.  I was mounted and when the sun was down I fired my pistol, the torches were applied and all of us retired to a safe distance to witness the fireworks and the explosions began, and such fire-works I have never seen since, though I have seen many.  A whole car would seem to explode at once, others would seem almost to leave the ground whole and then explode filling the air around and sky above with exploding shells and cartridges, illuminating the heavens, with such deafening sounds as if the earth were suffering with volcanic explosion.  The Confederate Veteran of 1919, (Oct.) has a good picture of ruin of cars left there after their burning.

This was the knell of Atlanta, and could I have known what was to follow for the city and its people I should have paraphrased Macbeth's "hear it not oh my people, for 'tis a knell that sends thee to a hell of suffering."

After the evacuation of Atlanta I was detailed to Auburn, Ala., as Commandant of the Post where large hospitals were situated under Dr. D. D. Saunders, who made me his guest while there, this association with him having very great influence in shaping the events of my after life to be seen hereinafter.

While at Auburn, Wilson's raid from Montgomery, Ala., to Macon, Ga., occurred, and the hospitals were forced to flee, and I with them.  When we arrived at West Point, Ga., where the Chattahooche was to be crossed, I went to see Gen. R. C. Tyler, Commandant of the Post, whom I knew, to learn if he intended to defend the crossing.  He told me he was, and I offered my services which he accepted, making me his Adjutant for the day.  We went in the Fort with some 120 men for a whole day against some 3000 cavalry attacking, surrendering near nightfall after Gen. Tyler and twelve of defenders were killed.

This battle was on the 16th of April, 1865, some eight days after the surrender of General Lee, and was the last fight of the war East of the Mississippi. A detailed account of this engagement will be seen in my report of same, Con federate Veteran Aug. 1915. See "Last Battle of the War" page 157.

After surrender we were taken to Macon, Ga., where we arrived four days after, and then learned for the first time of the surrender. We were there paroled and this was the end of my soldier life.

The military annals of the Western Army detail the campaigns and battles of Cheatham's Division in all of which except Franklin I participated; and I recall many adventures and thrilling incidents of camp and battle, but to relate them would involve more of the ego of narration than I care to write. I prefer to leave the story of the "dangers I have passed" to what others may have said and written, and evidenced by the honors shown me by my surviving comrades, some of which will accompany this sketch.

Since the War I have been honored with appointments as Brigadier General, upon the Staffs of Generals Gordon, Evans, Walker, Van Zantz and, Commanders in Chief of the United Confederates and twice selected to deliver the annual address at Mobile and Macon, Ga.

The war being ended I returned home to find the plantation stripped of live stock and farming implements, the negroes free, and many of them gone, and nearly all business paralyzed. I determined to take charge of the plantation to relieve my father of this burden, and study law at the same time; but soon received a letter from my uncle—bv marriage —John B. Robinson, then living at Memphis, inviting me to come to his home in Memphis, live with him until I had been licensed as a lawyer, and advising me not to delay etc. I accepted at once, lived with him for some months in which I read the Junior and Sophomore studies of Lebanon Law School, and then entered the Senior class of 1866 and graduated in January 1867.

I have referred to the timely aid of Uncle Robinson in appreciation of its helpfulness, and to express my heartfelt gratitude and tribute to his loving gentleness of character. I have myself feelings of satisfaction that I was permitted in after years to repay in kind somewhat his timely helpfulness.

One of my class mates at Lebanon was a Confederate soldier, Horace H. Lurton, with whom I happily formed the warmest friendship which continued for over fifty years, followed with many meetings full of social pleasure, and in many acts of mutual helpfulness. I watched with pride his elevation first as Chancellor of his District, then Judge and Chief Justice of the Supreme Court of Tennessee, then U. S. Circuit Judge, and finally a Justice of the Supreme Court of the United States. Upon his last elevation he sent me his portrait in his robe of Justice, with this inscription,

"For my best and oldest friend, and there are no friends like the old ones, L. B. McFarland from his friend
                              Horace H. Lurton."

We were both stricken with heart failure, largely result of over exertion about the same time, and during the months of January and February, 1914, both were in Florida, he at Miami and I at Ormond. He learned I was at Ormond and joined me there and we spent several weeks together. My automobile was with us and we with our wives spent each afternoon on the beautiful beach of Ormond; riding from Ormond to mouth of Halifax River, on one side the sea waves beating to our ear, singing the sad song the sea sings forever, while the sun sank behind the moaning pines on the other.

We parted to meet the coming summer, if living. When the summer came he went to Atlanta Beach and wrote me to join him, but before I could do so he died suddenly.

After leaving Lebanon Law School with license to practice law, I returned to Memphis and entered the office of Mr. J. M. Gregory, then in fine practice, and remained with him for about a year, under the most pleasing of association and resulting in intimate friendship with himself and family. I then opened an office myself and gradually obtained a lucrative practice.

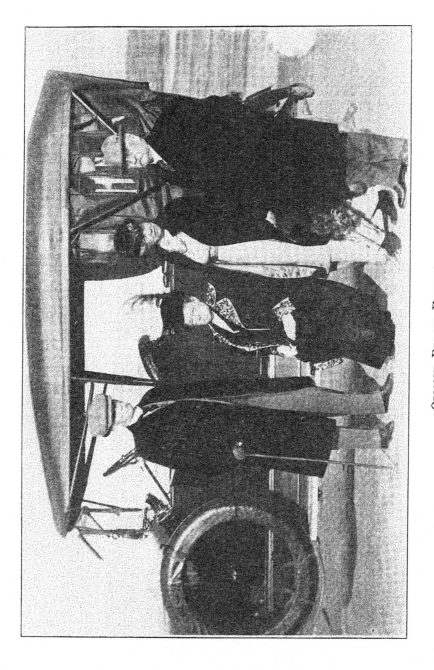

ORMOND BEACH FLORIDA.

Left to r

In 1880, Judge Robert J. Morgan, who had been our chancellor for a number of years, quit the bench and we formed a partnership which continued until 1890, when he retired on account of ill health and died shortly afterwards. I could not express too highly my appreciation of his congenial partnership, his pleasant companionship as a lawyer and man, his nobility of character and worth as friend and citizen.

In 1880, through influence of Gen. John C. Brown, then connected with the Missouri Pacific system, and army friend of both Judge Morgan and myself, our firm was made Attorneys of the St. Louis, Iron Mountain & Southern Railroad Company, then contemplating running into Memphis, and we represented that road from this date to Judge Morgan's death, and after his death I continued attorney for all of the Gould roads in Memphis, including St. Louis, Iron Mountain Railroad, the Cotton Belt, and then when the Iron Mountain Railroad Company of Memphis was chartered became a director here and attorney of this, also Vice President of the Union Railway. The organization of this road, a Belt Line, and obtaining right of way around Memphis involved great labor and a large amount of litigation in condemnation and defense of damage suits involving large amounts and many legal questions of eminent domain.

During this period I became acquainted with Mr. Jay Gould, and after his death his son George Gould, the first and one of the most remarkable and foresighted men I have ever known. During my connection with these railroads, the Gould System, I was fortunate in serving under able and appreciative chiefs, General Solicitors of the Missouri Pacific System, and finally Hon. Alexander G. Cochran became our chief as Vice President and General Attorney of the system, and for many years, and until my retirement from practice our service under him was most pleasant, and my personal relations the most cordial and friendly. In fact his consideration, kindness and friendship was the most pleasing of any of my professional life; and my retirement was protested by him both in person and by letter. Fortunately, however, he is still living honored and beloved, and our personal relations of friendship still enjoyed by me.

After twenty-eight years of service with this system, and forty-one years of practice, in 1908 I retired from the practice of the law, not wishing to "lag superfluous" or suffer suspicion of waning strength, and wishing to pass the balance of my days in the serene enjoyment of the fuller companionship of my wife, my home, my library and other of the many points of life I had purposely taught myself to touch looking to this period.

During my professional career I had no aspiration for political promotion. This was one of the rules of conduct I early fixed to follow. However, in 1895, the United States Attorney for Memphis District died, Mr. Justice Howell E. Jackson, then one of the Judges of the Supreme Court of the United States, and having the appointment of *ad interim* successor, sent me a commission as United States Attorney. This was without my application or previous knowledge. Mr. Justice Jackson was then on his death bed, and this commission signed by him which I still have, is probably the last official signature of his.

I did not, however, accept the office.

I was also commissioned several times as one of the judges of the Supreme Court of Tennessee to sit, as provided by law, in place of one of the regular judges, unable to sit from some cause, to hear separate cases, or for a term.

Among others, in 1896 to hear *Prewitt* v. *Bunch* (100 Tenn. 723) at Nashville, and in 1899, for a term at Jackson, Tenn., and some of the opinions delivered by me are found in 102 and 103 Tenn. Reports.

One of the points of life and its pleasures touched and sedulously cultivated and intensely enjoyed was out of doors sports; a love of great nature, her fields and flowers, her streams, her broad prairies, her deep forests of towering trees and sylvan solitudes, conversing with nature and viewing her stores unrolled, which as the poet sings was not solitude to me. The love of fine horses and the cultivation of the soil, the mysterious transmigration of a minute seed to the golden glow of the waving grain in the summer's heat, was my inheritance and for years my rest from professional labor.

The first Tennessee bred and owned horse to trot under 2:10, "Turley" was reared on my Ellemac Farm. For three years he was on the Grand Circuit driven by "Pop Geers" and won many large purses and trophies including the much sought Walnut Hall Cup which now adorns my library—I finally sold Turley to Mr. Billings of New York who took him to Europe with other of his celebrated horses.

My recreation was out of doors, I loved to feel the bending rod, the humming reel, and the leaping bass. The excitement of chase of deer or fox with good horse and deep mouthed hounds had no equal. The wonderful intelligence, the assiduous activity and coolness, efforts of pointer or setter were delightful to watch; and the whir of quail, or the rush of grouse more stirred the blood than any city scenes, and I loved to look upon the faces of kindred spirits by the camp-fire's glow—to listen to their tales of field and chase, the wonderful work of their Gladstone and Pink B, and to tell of my Chuck and Gordon and Mack.

I have hunted and fished from Georgian Lake in Canada to Florida, including lakes of Minnesota, Arkansas, and the Gulf of Mexico from Biloxi to Fort Meyers, and helped to organize the sporting clubs of Beaver Dam, in Mississippi, and Oakdonic, afterwards named Hatchie Coon, and Waponocka in Arkansas.

My special hunting companions for a number of years were David Poston, Sam P. Walker, and Arthur Wheatly. Every Christmas week for six or eight years, we spent at our preserve near LaGrange, Tennessee, shooting quail; then we shot snipe and prairie chicken on the prairie in Arkansas, and when these became scarce we followed the chickens to Iowa, Minnesota, and the Dakotas, spending many September's in this sport, and until by their deaths I was left alone. These three were ardent sportsmen, genial companions, and warm friends, whose death each came too soon and were deeply deplored by me.

After their deaths my hunting companion for years was Dr. J. M. Madden of Nashville, member of our Waponocka Club.

Each year on the opening of the season for prairie chicken, found us, my wife, our companion at Minneapolis, Minn., ready to start for some point for a month's shooting. Spirit Lake, Iowa, Webster's, South Dakota, or Cheyenne, North Dakota, near Devil's Lake and Canada.

One year we shot on Niobrara River, Nebraska. In these hunts we took with us our two best dogs each, located at best hotel in some small town, engaged two horse drag and driver, started at seven o'clock each morning and drove for a few miles, turned loose two dogs at a time and followed these over the new harvested wheat fields, no fences, and immense prairie; our dogs ranging broadly one on each side, sometimes nearly a mile away but in sight, and then when one found a covey would stand staunchly until we reached them when we would descend from our vehicle and flush the birds.

At noon we would seek shade at nearest and most inviting homestead, eat our lunch and rest for a couple of hours.

Then the evening sport, and as the sun would set we would call the dogs in and they would soon be asleep at our feet, and we drove for home, sometimes ten miles away— and such a drive; the rolling prairie, its views of splendid distances, breathing pure and exhilarating air—very elixir to our lungs.

In one of these rests the docter lay down in the shade of the drag and he and his "twa dogs" took their noon nap together. Floy, my wife, took the jug we carried water in for self and dogs, placed it at the doctor's head and with the sign, "Gone to the Dogs," as if he were drunk, and we watched for his waking, after taking photo of the scene.

Our last hunt together was on Cheyenne River, North Dakota.

MRS. FLOY McFARLAND—DR. MAD EN.

MRS. ELLEN SAUNDERS McFARLAND.

The Little Rebel.

The spring following the dear old doctor died at his home in Nashville, and we never cared to go again to the scenes of many glorious days of outing.

A more ardent sportsman, genial companion, true friend and noble tender-hearted gentleman never lived.

My social and home life has been one of the special blessings, due principally to my having twice found in marriage

"That happy communion which links
What woman feels purely with
What man nobly thinks."

I have referred herein to my reception at Auburn by Dr. Dudly D. Saunders, then in charge of a number of hospitals at Auburn, Alabama, and his fleeing with his hospitals before Wilson's Calvary. He had gotten across the Chattahooche River at West Point with his hospitals and he remained there and witnessed from an elevation, the defense of Fort Tyler.

When Dr. Saunders returned to the Saunders homestead, Rocky Hill, Ala., he related to the family the story of this West Point battle, and incidently related the part I had taken, doubtless coloring much from friendly feeling to my credit, and said to his young sister Ellen Virginia, the "Little Rebel," that he wanted her to know me.

He returned to Memphis and subsequently invited Ellen to visit them. She came, I saw, and she conquered, and a lengthy courtship followed. My fate hung in the balance until I think an address that I made to the Confederates in 1871, published in the Appeal swung the balance in my favor.

"She loved me for the dangers I had passed,
And I loved her that she did pity them."

We were married at Rocky Hill on the 4th of April, 1872, by Bishop Robert Paine.

I was immediately adopted by the Saunders family and numerous branches of kin.

Rocky Hill, the Saunders homestead near Courtland, Ala., was a stately mansion of many rooms, crowning a hill that overlooked a large plantation, a model southern home.

The family then consisted of Col. James E. Saunders and wife Mary, *nee* Watkins; their daughter Ellen Virginia; a grand daughter Elizabeth (daughter of Mary Louise Saunders, who married Henry D. Blair of Mobile, Ala., both of whom died leaving her then an orphan quite young).

Others members of the family then living, but not with them, were Dr. Dudly Saunders, Robert Turner Saunders and Mrs. Sarah Hayes, *nee* Saunders.

The Saunders were related to many of the most extensive and distinguished families of Alabama and Mississippi. Bishop Robert Paine and the Banks, Billups and Bradfords of Mississippi; the Watkins, Harris, and Sherrods of Alabama, and many others.

Col. James E. Saunders was one of the best type of southern gentlemen, manly in form, courtly in manner, cultured and learned, one of the distinguished men of the South for many years.

Served on the staff of Gen. Bedford Forrest, and desperately wounded at capture of Murfreesboro. He lived to the age of ninety-one years, and gently passed away at Rocky Hill, Aug. 31, 1896.

His wife was an embodiment of all the higher virtues of wife, mother, hostess and Christian.

The grand-daughter, Elizabeth Blair, married W. C. Stubbs, Ph. D., of distinguished Virginia family, professor in the Agricultural School of Alabama and Louisiana, and recognized as one of the most distinguished agriculturists of the South.

Mrs. Stubbs is a lovely character, highly cultivated, and literary in taste and habit. Her grandfather, Col. Saunders, had in his years of three score and ten, written for his county paper, a valuable and interesting history of the early settlers of Alabama. After his death Mrs. Stubbs gathered these together for editing which she did.

This was followed by a biography by her grandfather and mother. To this she added notes and genealogies of the families of Saunders and their kin far and near, some two hundred pages, one of the most painstaking and complete of any genealogical work extant.

This family was in itself with three beautiful and bright girls, and the Col. and Mother Saunders, an interesting circle; and when the doctor and his wife Mary Saunders, *nee* Wheatly, and daughter Kate, and sometimes with Mrs. Weaver, stepmother of Mrs. Dr. Saunders, were added to the circle, the days of Rocky Hill were days of sunshine, and the evenings were *noctes embrosianae,* and the table talk especially a constant scintillation of fun and frolic, wisdom and wit, and quick repartee. And our home and Dr. Saunders' in Memphis enjoyed for years the same family meetings and social pleasurers with same sparkling wit and lightning repartee.

Dr. Dudly Saunders was one of the noblest men I have ever known, loved and honored by all who knew him. He was in every way a congenial companion, hospitable at home, a lover of out of door sports, splendid shot, a master of chess and one of the ablest of his profession, tender and sympathetic. He became a brother to me, and his death was one of the greatest losses I have ever sustained.

Immediately after our marriage and return to Memphis we were called to Jackson, Tennessee, in attendance upon the Supreme Court of Tennessee then in session, and spent the most of that term there.

I shall always remember with pride and deep appreciation the courteous welcome my brothers of the bench and bar gave us and the tribute of attention they gave my wife.

In those days the lawyers of Memphis were closely attached to each other and carefully observant of social duties. My young wife gifted by nature, entertaining by culture, and of quick wit and charming manner, entertained with ease, and her parlor was nightly filled with judges of the court and my brother members of the bar.

After some years of ambitions, hopes, the endearment of many friends, the happiness of a congenial home, followed by several years of sickness and pain she passed away on the 30th of June, 1900. The Commercial Appeal of July 1, 1900, had the following notice of her death:

### DEATH OF MRS. McFARLAND.

"Mrs. Ella McFarland, the wife of Judge L. B. McFarland, died yesterday morning at an early hour at the family residence, 364 Linden Street. Mrs. McFarland had been ill for a protracted period, and her death was not unexpected. She suffered from a pulmonary trouble and bore her sickness with great fortitude to the last. She was about 55 years of age and was one of the best known matrons in Memphis—a brilliant woman by culture and a gifted one by nature. Her married life, covering a period of thirty years, was a happy one, and numerous friends sympathize with her husband in his bereavement. No children survive her, though she leaves many relatives. She was Miss Ella Saunders, a daughter of the late Col. Saunders, and a sister of Dr. D. D. Saunders of this city. The funeral services will take place from the residence this afternoon at 5 o'clock. Rev. Dr. Robert Mahon pastor, of the Central Methodist Church, will conduct the services. The interment will occur at Elmwood."

(*Commercial Appeal, July 1, 1900.*)

She sleeps now in Elmwood Cemetery and the monument erected to her memory bears this inscription:

"A steadfast friend, a dutiful daughter, a loyal and loving wife,
Awakening appreciation of the poetic and beautiful in life,
And inspiring to noble thoughts and worthy ambition.
Writ by one who knew her best and loved her most."

After several years of loneliness, I married Mrs. Floy G. Allen, widow of Thos. H. Allen, Jr. She was the daughter of Barnett Graham and Sarah Anderson.

Barnett Graham came to Memphis from Greensboro, North Carolina, on horseback, when he was sixteen years of age. He grew in importance as a citizen and benefactor to Memphis as he grew in stature. He served the city as alderman, as did then the best of citizens, in 1837-38.

He accumulated a fine fortune. He built the first brick store in Memphis, at the southwest corner of Main and Gayoso, now owned and occupied by the Goldsmiths, and other store houses on Main, which he traded for negroes some years before the Civil War. He also owned several hundred acres of land in the suburbs, then, including the present Elmwood Cemetery, and the beautiful grounds now occupied by the Methodist Hospital, upon which he built a handsome brick residence, a part of which still remains, which he and his family occupied during his life, and his family for years after his death, until this and his estate passed to others, the not unusual fate of accumulated fortunes left to incompetent survivors.

His daughter, Floy, was born and grew up in this house, and the street adjoining on the east, given by her father, was named Florence for her. He died on the seventh day of August, 1866, aged fifty-five, and the then newspaper of Memphis paid him a lengthy tribute of which the following is a part:

"He came from North Carolina, the 'land of steady habits,' and brought with him those characteristic traits of the good old state that distinguished her sons everywhere. His uniform, steady and unremitting attention to business was the genius of his success. His manner was quiet and demure, and few knew how much true worth and genuine good feeling lay hidden beneath an exterior that was devoid of demonstration. To know him in his true character, you had to become intimately acquainted with him. Accustomed from his youth to depend upon himself alone, he acquired habits of silence and reserve that was in keeping with his temperament. He was an exceedingly modest man, and was ever averse to anything that severed of display.·

He was liberal without ostentation. He went about doing good for the sake of the good it would render others, without any pharisaic thought of himself; hence his charities were only known to the immediate beneficiaries, and their name is legion. It has been said that the world knows not its greatest men. This saying is admirably adapted to him. But a short time ago and the whole South was up in arms calling for help. There were many who went about talking much and doing little. Mr. Graham was slow to move in the matter, but when he gave to the cause, his donations numbered thousands, while others, less stable and more ready, gave their ten. There are moral heroes as well as political and military, and he was one. Though he never professed any particular creed, yet in his dealings with men he was ever deemed an honest man, the noblest work of God."

Floy's mother was a daughter of Nathaniel Anderson, another of the pioneer settlers of Memphis, and closely identified with its youthful growth, and participated with M. B. Winchester, Isaac Rawlings, and others of the prominent citizens, in the organization of the city on April 26, 1827, under the Charter of 1826, and served himself as one of its aldermen in 1827-1828. He was also first president of the Merchants Bank.

His sons and grandsons served in four wars—ten in the Confederate army.

Mrs. Graham, Floy's mother, was a beautiful woman, in fact, a belle in her young womanhood and noted all her life for her generous charity and gracious hospitality. She died on the 14th day of March, 1886, and she and her husband rest in Elmwood.

Floy and I were married on the first day of September, 1902, in the beautiful little Episcopal Church at Sewanee, Tennessee, by Bishop Thos. F. Gailor.

The best tribute I can properly pay to her is to say that no other woman more companionable to me than she has been, could have been won nor more blest could I have been

MRS. FLOY GRAHAM McFARLAND.

that she has survived so many years that have passed since we were wedded.

My closing sentence, here uttered in profound gratitude, is that of the psalmist—"Surely, goodness and mercy have followed me all the days of my life."

# COMMEMORATION DAY.

MEMPHIS, MAY 6TH, 1871. CEREMONIES AT ELMWOOD CEMETERY—
A LARGE CONGREGATION GO OUT TO STREW THE GRAVES OF
THE HEROIC DEAD WITH FLOWERS.

———

The Ceremonies—Poems Recited on the Occasion—
Oration by Mr. McFarland.

———

(*From the Daily Appeal, May 7.*)

\*  \*  \*  \*  \*  \*  \*

Then came the oration of the day, by Mr. McFarland. It was listened to throughout with great attention and frequent murmurs of applause.

### THE ORATION.

Suppose some wanderer from a distant sphere, a stranger to our history, our customs and the impulses by which we are swayed, should be a visitant among us, and present here to-day. Seeing this vast throng his interest would be awakened, his curiosity excited and he would ask, at once, the meaning of this grand and solemn, yet simple pageant.

He would be told that a decade of years since a fierce civil war was joined between the Northern and Southern sections of this country; that armies were marshaled, marches made, sieges endured and battles fought. It raged fiercely for four years, and during its continuance, thousands of the best citizen soldiery perished. Their remains gathered from bivouac and battle-field, were buried here and now, each year, the survivors of this terrible war—maimed comrades of the battle plain and grief stricken hearts of the hearth stone, youth and age, maid and matron, son and sire—all come to deck their quiet graves with wreaths and garlands of evergreen and bouquets of flowers, to commemorate the glorious deeds of the fallen, to transmit their excellences and perpetuate their virtues.

He would be told that in addition to the simple rite of strewing flowers, some one, usually a renowned soldier, an illustrious statesman, an able advocate or an eloquent panegyrist; sometimes, though only a simple citizen, with neither wit nor wisdom nor the power of speech, whose only recommendation is in having sympathized with the cause, becomes the speaker of the hour and voices the mingled pride and grief of the assembled throng.

It would be explained to him how, seeking other-forms of expression, this people would soon rear a monument, sublime in conception, grand in proportion and perfect in execution, to the memory of the dead. Hearing these things, methinks our visitor, impressed with the tenderness of the scene and the sublime sentiments of the people, without pausing to inquire into the causes of the war or seeking to discover which of the contending parties was right and which wrong, would exclaim at once· "Glorious are the living, whose impulses prompt such tributes as those, and more glorious still the dead, the memory of whose lives and virtues you thus perpetuate."

The custom of thus coming year by year within the hallowed precincts of the tomb and communing with the dead, is not only a proper homage to them, but also powerful for good to the living. Death, whether it come amid the bustle of the morn or at the gentle twilight; whether it whispers with the insidious salutations of disease, or trumps the soldier to a soldier's grave, in whichever of its protean shapes it comes, is a great teacher and humanitarian.

It reminds us of our mortality, weakness and dependence, and brings into active exercise all those sweet sympathies of our nature, which are the real ties binding society. It teaches youth, manhood and age lessons of wisdom. It teaches pride humility; meanness generosity, and gives to the sceptical faith. It tames the passions, subdues vanity, tempers ambition, refines the emotions, and sheds the softening glow of charity over all the deeds of our fellow men.

It teaches the earnest searcher for truth to exclaim as did Zanoni· "Through death is the only knowledge of all truth," or as was written upon the portals of the palace of Vathek, "this is the asylum of pilgrims, the refuge of travelers and the depository of secrets for all parts of the world."

We come to read some of these lessons of the tomb to-day. And let us not come as those who mourn without comfort, but rather with emotions of pride, drowned grief and emulous resolves; more in the spirit of the Thracians who wept at a birth and rejoiced at a funeral.

There is a deep philosophy in this which the selfish emotions of grief will not let us understand, or the passing pleasures of the present permit us to appreciate. It is the part of wisdom to accept that philosophy which reconciles with seeming misfortune.

It was not always that death wore the sombre hue of melancholy, or waked the wailings of grief. The ancients contemplated death without fear and met it with indifference.

In the beautiful fables of their religion Death was but the daughter of Night and the sister of sleep.

By them no emotions of horror were associated with their burial places. Their scarcophagi were sculptered with battles and the memorable actions of their heroes.

The Greeks called a burial ground Cemeterion, or "the sleeping place;" the Jews Bethshaim, or "the house of the living;" and the Germans Gottsfeld—"God's field." The Scriptures, themselves, speak only of the "Angel of Death."

It was not until much later, when monkish superstition had corrupted the beauty and simplicity of Christianity, that mankind first beheld the grave yawn, and "gaunt death in the Gothic form of human anatomy paraded the universe."

In this place, and on this occasion, grief should give way to pride for the death-crowned life of the dead. The soft Lydian and Ionian harmonies are not in unison with the place. The manly Dorian and heroic Phrygian should verse the praises of the heroic dead. And, if we bend low above the once proud forms which slumber here, while we scatter those flowers, we will also commune with their noble spirits, learn the grand impulses of their lives, and. catch the inspiration of their souls.  When we repeat the story of their heoric daring, their devotion, their patriotism, self-sacrifice and immolation, virtues we are here to-day to commemorate, and by that commemoration perpetuate, it is more for the living than the dead.  And, as the Grecian youths heard from the Parthenon the story of Marathon and Thermopylæ, and the Roman saw daily in the Atrium the statues of his illustrious ancestors, his heart was fired with a noble emulation. . So do we trust these memorial services and the honors bestowed upon our dead, may cause the youth of our land to emulate their virtues.

The paying of some public tribute to those who have devoted their lives to their country, has been common to most nations; the form and manner of its expression depending in each age upon the education, culture and refinement of the people.

Valor in arms has, in every age and with every nation, claimed the warmest attention and elicited the most excited plaudits.  And when this disregard of danger is coupled with sacrifice of self for principles of religion or love of country, it is held "as the chiefest virtue and most dignifies the haver."

It is the saying of an Eastern poet that a valiant camel driver is worthy to kiss the lips of a fair queen; while a cowardly prince is not worthy to salute the hem of her garments.

The pronouncing of eulogies in their honor was instituted by Athenians just after the Samian war, which was, as this, a civil war; the judges of the Areopagus appointing the speaker for each occasion, the tribute thus coming with all the authority of a decree from the lips of Justice herself.

Lycurgus, regulating the affairs of the Lacedæmonian, had the soldiers buried near the temples of the gods, and would not permit the names of any to be inscribed upon tombs, but those who had fallen in battle.

Pictures were painted in honor of Miltiades, and while living, three hundred statues were erected to Demetrius. The Chinese also sacrifice to the spirit of their illustrious dead.

During the wars of Napoleon there was in one of the French grenadier regiments a soldier, La Tour d'Auvergne, conspicuous at all times for his gallantry, and who was finally killed in battle.

For a number of years there was witnessed a beautiful custom in his regiment commemorating his heroism. Each day when the company was assembled for parade and the roll was called, there was one name to which its owner could not answer. It was that of d'Auvergne. When it was called, the oldest sergeant present stepped a pace forward, raised his hand to his cap, and said proudly: "Died on the field of honor." With how many of us, and how often does memory call the names of our dead, to be answered: "Died on the field of honor." For a number of years the brave but peaceful Swiss were accustomed to scatter flowers upon the graves of their dead upon the battlefield of Morganta and Laupen. No tribute could be more expressive than this of strewing flowers—flowers, "the fugitive poetry of nature"—her "pater noster and the forget-me-nots of affection." It is stamped with woman's nature. She only could have thought of it. Its simplicity, beauty, delicacy and refinement make it peculiarly hers.

It is not statues and monuments or magnificent obsequies that attest at all times a nation's gratitude.

Tributes like these only are enduring. Tacitus gracefully says, "the sighs and tears of a people are the most permanent and enduring statues; they are not obnoxious to the inclemencies of the weather or the injuries of time, and endear the memory of the good and virtuous to the remotest ages."

But we have said we speak to-day for the present and to the living. The Past—the tearful, blood-stained, robe-enwrapped past—is gone, and will not come again. The active Present is upon us, and is ours; and the glorious Future, at whose portals we stand, catching the light glowing from within, opens before us. It is with these and their high and holy duties we must grapple. The past is to be remembered but for its solemn sacrifices, its potent lessons. For these it is valuable. It is the great teacher. Upon ·its altars lie the smoking victims from which true divination must come, and its oracles, if read aright, will be more truthful than those of Jupiter Ammon to Alexander, less dubious than those of Delphi to Crœsus.

One of the lessons which it teaches, and one which will give us consolation and hope to remember, is that the seeming misfortune of individuals and the apparent calamities of nations are ofttimes the means of their greatest good.

By some law, incomprehensible to us, adversity, suffering and death are the most potent agencies for the accomplishment of good. "Perfect through suffering" is a great truth, a sublime mystery. It is writ in the chart of this life inseparable from this being. And, as in the delightful gardens of Maumal, famous for its fruits and its flowers, its rivulets and its fountains, above all its vernal beauty the cypress waved, and mingled its low, monotone miserere with the song of birds and fall of waters; so in all the walks of this life, the cypress waves above the orange boughs, though its blooms are fresh for the brow of the bride.

But there is good in all this. It is an Eastern saying that adversity is like the period of the former and latter rains —cold, comfortless, unfriendly to man and beast, yet from that season have their birth the fruit, the flowers, the date, the rose and the pomegranate.

As with individuals so with nations, the period of their adversity is the germinating period of their greatness. The beautiful isles of the ocean are the children of the earthquake, or the graves of the coral. From the throes of a revolution is often born a giant nation. A people too prosperous become effeminate anl licentious, when their land is overrun by a more hardy race, who take the place of the weak, and a new march of prosperity begins.

Through war the Norman was engrafted upon the Saxon, and an English people with all their noble characteristics was the result.

Through its memorable struggles, most of them civil dissensions, and many religious controversies—York against Lancaster, Tudor against Stewart, Protestant against Papist, Dissenter against Churchman, Roundhead against Cavalier, and of jealous Baron against royal oppression, we have the charters of right, an English Parliament and an English Constitution.

The crusades caused millions to perish abroad, and famine and pestilence to reign at home; but the most beneficial effects resulted from these apparent calamities—among these, it destroyed the influence of Germanic royalty, erected by Pepin and Charlemagne, upon the ruins of Rome. Its expenditures impoverished the nobles and their immense domains were divided and sold, by which agriculture, trade, commerce and individual independence and enterprise were fostered and encouraged.

The French revolution of 1792 was a bloody and tearful chapter in history, but who will now deny its salutary effects. And we doubt not the French revolution of the present—the disasters of Sedan and Metz—the humiliation of Paris, and the now occurring horrors of the Tuileries and the Bois de Bologne, are but the agencies of some great good yet, in the years to come, to flow from these apparent calamities.

Wars rage, armies meet in the shock of battle, and millions perish in the smoke of conflict. Republics dissolve and empires fall, but at each commotion and each ebb of the tide, man is left higher and higher upon the mighty shores of the sea of his existence. It is by the lightning's flash, playing in lambent flames around the evening horizon or leaping luridly through the sky, the air is kept pure. Its efficacy must not be denied because to some it is the swift messenger of death. 'Tis by commotion—

—"When the winds
Take the ruffian billows by the top
Curling their monstrous heads and
hanging them
With deafening clamors in the slip-
pery clouds"

that the waters of the sea are purified. Storms must not abate because in their wild wrath an unfortunate ship must go down.

We venture to assert that to the careful reader of history it is apparent that in most instances the good which resulted to mankind at large from wars, more than counterbalanced the evils to the generations that suffered them.

Nor is this an argument for their encouragement. We do not mean that the same good results might not have been accomplished by other agencies, could they have been put in motion. War sometimes becomes the healthful medicine to the diseased bodies politic. The study of the statesman and the care of the philanthropist is to avoid or remove its causes, which are wrongs and oppression. So long as these exist, in the absence of some international forum, some scheme of national arbitration, appeals to the sword must remain a necessary evil.

And, we may here remark, that already do we see European publicists and statesmen citing our war and its results as affording a solution of the difficulties in the way of a federation of nations and the abolition of wars, and especially as precluding any future wars on this continent.

With these records of the past and others we need not here repeat, we do no violence to reason when we suggest that, instead of a calamity, the late war will, in the aggregate, prove more beneficial to the South—certainly to mankind at large—than if it had never occurred; or more than if victory had perched upon our banners. You and I, and this genera-tion, suffering the immediate consequences, may not see or appreciate the full effects of it, but we doubt not that the time will come when the suffering of these people will fructify in great good to our race, develop itself in a higher civilization, a more perfect government and greater freedom.

"War is not always an evil; it sometimes restores the brotherhood of men and States in letters of fire."

And we do no dishonor to the dead when we thus speak. It is often that the death of the brave and the great, though by violence and wrong, is more potent for good to their fellowman than their whole lives, however spent, could have been. The death of the patriot, though in defeat, often accomplishes more than his living, through success, could have done. 1236219

Who can fathom the unscrutable ways of Providence? The blood of the martyr is the seed of the church; and above the graves of a country's heroes there hovers the spirit of a country's liberties.

"There is grandeur in graves; there is glory in gloom." A people are never truly patriotic, and never cling with the tenderness of children to a land until that land is dotted with the graves of its heroic dead; until its history, romance and poetry glow with the deeds of their daring. Without traditions, heroes and graves binding men to a spot, all the earth and sky are to them alike.

He who looks not hopefully at the future of our country forgets the lessons of the past; his reason is but time-serving, and cannot rise above the influences of the hour and the sway of his prejudices. In spite of her many civil wars, and the repeated disregard of her constitutional privileges by usurping monarchs, England is to-day united, free, prosperous and great. With France the sun of Austerlitz rose gloriously upon her "Old Guards," glinting back their bayonets gleam and the scream of her victorious eagles was heard upon the banks of the Danube, the Boristhenes and the Po, long after the civil dissensions of Catholic and Protestant, of Navarre and Valois, and of the 9th Thermidor. So with the Netherlands, and so with Germany, Italy and Spain.

The conquests of Alexander through bloody battles planted Greek settlements and cities in every country he conquered and blended its civilization, literature and science with that of the conquered and not many years after he crossed the Hellespont the Greek language was spoken in Egypt and from the Aegean to the Indies.

The evils, social and political, we experience to-day are but of the present. Ere many years the people of both North and South, whose great heart, we believe, if understood, beats in unison to the march of prosperity, will rise in their majesty and hurl those who have been and are guilty of oppression and constitutional infraction from power, and a new era of prosperity for our whole country will begin.

If contest there must ever be again between the two sections, let it be in the Congress of the whole nation, in the marts of trade, the halls of learning, the domain of science, and the cultivation of the arts. Then mayhap the victory will be ours, and it repeated of us as of Greece when Rome had bound her fast:

"The beautiful captive wound her charms around the barbarous captor, and held him in subjection to a vassalage infinitely more glorious than all his universal power and boasted mastery in arms."

Think not that, because the immediate objects for which these suffered and died was not attained, their loss is not recompensed. Nothing good is ever lost. A great, generous thought, a heroic deed, a glorious action, can never die. Though deep buried in the earth, after long years the seed ripens into a harvest, *"Dormit aliquando jus, moritur nuquam."* Things material perish. The monuments of skill, evidences of taste, and characteristics of genius fade, but the worthy creations of the intellect, the grand inspirations of the soul are immortal. Babylon and Persepholis, the stately columns of the Coliseum and the sculptured pillars of the Pantheon all crumble to ruins. "The spider weaves his web in the imperial palace, and the owl sings his solitary watch song upon the towers of Arasiab;" but the prowess of Diomed, the sacrifice of Iphigenia, the philosophy of Plato and Aristotle and the verses of Homer made them immortal. Who can tell the lasting influence of the life and death of great, good men upon the history of a nation and of ages. Though dead their spirit still pervades the universe. Their presence is felt still in the councils of their people, and in the times of their adversity their names are pillars of strength against which all lean.

The beautiful, the good and the heroic of every age are always garnered for the future.

"I know not how; some grains of wheat
That thirty centuries had been
Confined beneath a mummy's feet,
In a new world shot fresh and sweet;
And the young crop of living green
Grew golden in the summer's heat."

It was these glorious deeds, and their sacrifices, the age and their country demanded; our country needed the times just past for the time which is to come. It needed its bitter experience, its struggles, its courage, its endurance and self-sacrifice. Without these it would, perhaps, have been unprepared to fill its mission in the destiny of nations.

Yesterday was our autumn of chilling winds and falling leaves; our germinating winter of clouds and storms and snows. To-day is the springtime with its bursting buds and all the palpitating energies of active life, and to-morrow it will be a summer of golden grain, when the reapers will be wanted. No period of history—no era in a country's growth or greatness—ever saw the time when such experience and such examples were more needed. That they should have so come, each in their season, and that it should have so happened, seems but a part of that divine economy which, when space was undefined and darkness was upon the face of the deep, said "let there be light," and there was light.

We are just now entering upon an era in which all of those elements of greatness, so conspicuous in our soldiers, will be most needed in our people.

The everlasting war between liberty and despotism, knowledge and ignorance is yet raging. With the growth of empires and nations, notwithstanding the experience of ages, human government remains the most complicated of sciences. In the increase of trade and extension of commerce, political economy and the adaptation of the laws to the wants and consciences of men, becomes the mort important of studies, and in the advancement of the sciences and cultivation of the arts, individual education and culture must' command the most serious attention.

Nor must the private virtues of individuals be neglected. The welfare of nations depends upon the private character of its individuals. Totilla, the Goth, was in the habit of saying that "public vice and public ruin went hand in hand."

The old war between good and evil is still being fought. The fable of Ormuzd and Ahriman is as true to-day as when the Chaldean worshiped his orb of gold. It is as necessary to the purity and perpetuity of our institutions that private morals be inculcated as that political economy should be studied. And it is fortunate for us of the South—fortunate for the time that is, and the years and generations that are to come—that the private virtues of the central figures of this revolution were as conspicuous as their military genius and public worth. We see now why the finger of destiny pointed them to the pedestal of fame.

The immediate future is to be a time of grand designs, stupendous undertakings, and many noble deeds.

It will be especially an age of activity. The human mind must expand to embrace all the realms of knowledge, and human energy must be equal to the appointed tasks. He must

"Live in deeds, not years; in thoughts,
    not breaths;
In feelings, not in figures on a dial.
We should count time by heart throbs.
    He most lives
Who thinks most, feels the noblest, acts
    the best."

It is then, in conclusion, for ourselves, for the present and future glory of our country that the memory of our heroic dead is priceless.

Let their virtues be perpetuated by costly statues, storied urn and monumental shaft. Let History come with her scroll, painting her canvas, and sculpture her chisel, and transmit their many virtues to the remotest ages.

But above all and beyond all of these—nearer and dearer than all else—each year, as spring returns with her morns of roses, her evenings radiant smiles, her valleys robe-folded in green and her breast bouquet gardens of flowers; let woman, in all her constancy and tenderness and truth, come to this hallowed spot, as at evening the stars steal in God's temple to worship, and with her sighs and tears build her monuments to the dead, more enduring than marble.

### EDITORIAL.
#### (*Daily Appeal, May* 10, 1871.)

The honors paid to the Confederate dead at Elmwood Saturday, indicated that time, misfortunes and persecutions have only increased and intensified the devotion of the Southern people to their slain sons. Interesting as the ceremonies have heretofore been, and large as the attendance has been hitherto, the ceremonies have never been so interesting or the crowd so large as that of yesterday. The immense concourse of people and the general manifestation of sympathy and respect for the dead, showed that our people will never forget the glory and grandeur of the late struggle, nor the deeds of the men whose heroic achievements won the admiration of the world. The ceremonies lasted from eight o'clock in the morning until sundown. While there were not more than six or eight thousand people on the ground at any one time, we feel safe in saying that no less than twenty thousand people visited the cemetery during the day. There was a steady and continuous stream pouring in and out of the different gates. Carriages, buggies and street cars loaded with living compact masses, dashed along the thoroughfares, while on the roads were ladies, men and children walking singly or

in little groups, but all traveling to a common destination.
Every pilgrim bore a floral offering. The ladies in charge
of the decoration, headed by Mrs. Cummings, performed their
duties with fidelity and displayed a taste which was highly
commended by all. The full particulars of the commemora
tion services will be found in our columns; and we cannot
close this hasty notice of these sad yet impressive memorial
rites without congratulating the orator of the day, L. B. Mc-
Farland, Esq., on his success. He is young in years, but the
field was wide, the theme inspiring and the occasion gave
ample scope for his eloquence and genius, and he was equal
to his opportunities. We publish Mr. McFarland's oration in
full, and a perusal will show that his style unites a severe
simplicity with the requisite warmth of fancy and affluence
of diction. He is a young man of rare gifts, and we believe
this first great effort of his life has made for him a name
which is destined to achieve a brilliant fame.

# THE FRENCH BAR.

The following is the full text of Judge L. B. McFarland's paper read before the recent meeting of the Tennessee Bar Association at Bon Aqua.

## THE FRENCH BAR.
### (*Appeal, July 22, 1883.*)

When the French Bar first presented itself as a subject suitable for this occasion, its chief recommendation was that little was known about it even to the most general of American readers. A more mature consideration, however, of its history, discipline and influence suggested a higher use and nobler purposes in its treatment. The bar of France exemplifies in the highest degree the dignity, the power and the influence to which the bar of this country should and can attain by organization, coherence, education and discipline.

The same reason, however, that gives this subject interest from novelty, scarcity of authentic biographic and historic materials, adds greatly to the difficulty of its treatment. Some biographies of noted French advocates, some imperfect accounts of the rise, progress and present state of the French Bar, are accessible, but these do not suffice to give that which is most valuable. Mr. Buckle very justly remarks upon the inutility of mere biographic and historic narrative of events. Something higher and better than this is necessary, that the present and future may profit fully from the past; and it has often occurred that a fine field for philosophic treatment was now open to some Buckle or Draper or Lecky of the bar in discussing the influence of the bar upon the laws, the manners and the civilization of the world, or even of any particular country. But such a work would require the labor of a long life, the devotion of love, the inspiration of faith, and "the light of Genius directing the hand of industry." No imperfect sketch dotted hurriedly in the brief intervals of professional life can hope to reach this higher and more valuable plane of investigation.   Nor can more now be attempted than some remarks upon the French bar, mere twitterings of the swallows upon the temple of the gods.

### THE ANCIENT BAR OF FRANCE.

Was the successor of the bar of Rome, made illustrious by Cicero, Hortensius, Caesar and others of her celebrated orators and jurisconsults.   Even while Gaul was a Roman province the discipline and the eloquence of the Roman bar was transferred to the banks of the Seine and Garonne, and St. Jerome, Juvernal and Ansonius, chronicle the exuberance and brilliancy of Gallic eloquence, while Marcus Caesar and Domitius Afer disputed for the palm in the Roman forum, Quintillian mentions the latter as the finest orator he ever heard.   The Franks, however, swept away, in the resistless march of invasion, every vestige of Roman-Gallic jurisprudence, and the first mention we again have of the profession of the advocate was in the capitularies of Charlemagne, 802, ordaining that none should be admitted into the profession "but men mild, pacific, fearing God and loving justice." There is then a gap in the history until the finding of the Pandects at Amalfi, when the establishments of St. Louis appeared.   These were the work of a commission of learned jurisconsults, and the chapter on advocates provides, among other things, "that they shall never present an unjust case before a court, shall defend widows, orphans and the poor when required, and shall say nothing discourteously "   In 1327, Philip de Valois, then regent, promulgated several prescriptions, among others, requiring all advocates to take the oath and be inscribed on the roll of advocates, and providing that any advocate who shall have prevaricated in his duties shall be forever excluded from the court.   It also provides that advocates must be at the chatelet at the rising of the sun. This must have never been transferred to

### ENGLISH AND AMERICAN COURTS

or long since fallen in desuetude, else Blackstone would have never recommended to students the *"Viginti Annorum*

*Lucubrationes,"* or the late hours of lamp and office never
been enrolled among the habits of the modern lawyers. In
1344, by another regulation, a list was made of all the sworn
advocates, from which list the most capable shall be chosen
and sustained; the others shall be suspended. Other regula-
tions were established at different times, some of which are
especially worthy of notice. One divided advocates into three
classes: councillors, advocates, pleaders and listeners. The
first must have been ten years admitted. These wore a long
robe of black silk, covered with a scarlet mantle, lined with
ermine, and fastened on the chest with a rich clasp. The
pleaders wore a violet cloak, and the listeners a white one.
Exactly what part the listeners took in the administration of
justice we are not advised. Another regulation provided that
young advocates should be "respectful to their seniors; that
all should plead and write briefly; shall truly read without
omission, interruption or disguise; shall not proceed by injur-
ious words against the adverse party or advocate; must not
talk several at a time, or interrupt each other; shall not take
their seats except in decent attire; shall make no treaty with
their client depending on the event of the trial." This was
1344, and the first French ordinance against champerty, and
was derived from the Roman law. The modern definition
of champerty is, "A contract between client and attorney by
which, if the suit is lost, the client pays the costs; if won, the
attorney gets the recovery." Another and most important
regulation was early adopted, that requiring a time of proba-
tion—called "stage"—for young advocates to fit themselves
for their duties. This was not at first limited as to time, but
in 1490 it was provided that no one should be admitted to the
list of advocates who had not studied in a recognized university for five years, and found properly qualified.

It was not, however, until about 1690 that the bar attained its highest organization, when a complete roll of its
members was kept, admission to which was regulated by the
most stringent rules. The young candidate, who must be a
licentiate from the university and passed his state, was presented by one of the seniors of the bar, thus termed the god-
father of the applicant, and took the oath, after which his

name was inscribed upon the roll. This organization of the bar, by establishing a list with power of dismissal therefrom, continued, with few and short intervals of disorganization, until 1790, when the ancient French bar ceased to exist.

In this year the constituent assembly abolished the order of advocates.

### THE GOLDEN AGE

of French magistracy. Sequier, and Christopher de Thou were two of the most eminent advocates of the sixteenth century. The one brief and pointed in argument, the other diffuse and prolix, of one it was said *"Multa paucis,"* and of the other *"Pauca multis."* Budi, author of Commentaries of the Pandects, and styled "The Splendor and Ornament of the Realm, and the Restorer of the Roman Law," was also of the sixteenth century. He must likewise have been the Archimedes of his day, as it is related of him that being told that his house was on fire he simply said, "Tell my wife, I don't attend to such affairs," a reply not quite as sensible as that of the New Yorker, who received a telegram from his agent, saying, "Your house is on fire, what shall I do?" The answer was, "Put it out."

### DURING THE REIGN OF LOUIS XIV

the forum vied with the pulpit in eloquence and the stage in elegance. If Bossuet, Massillon and Bourdaloue gave splendor to the one, and Corneille and Racine adorned the other, Amur Tolue, Omer Talon Patru and Foucroy combined the splendors of oratory with the graces and elegance of poetry. The seventeenth century added many illustrious names to the list—Norman and Cochin, one the Hortensius and the other the Alcibiades of the French bar—while D'Agessau, and Pothier added additional worth and splendor to the legal literature of the age.

From the suspension of the roll and the functions of the advocates in 1790 until its restoration in 1800—ten years of social and political night and storm and darkness—there was no organized body of advocates, and nearly the entire roll refused to plead before the petty tribunals organized by the Constituent Assembly, for "amid the din of arms," as said Marius, "the laws spoke too softly to be heard." Another attorney was imprisoned with his son. The son was condemned but when the executioners came, the father answered to his name and took his place upon the scaffold.

### THE MODERN FRENCH BAR

dates from the reorganization of the roll in 1800. Napoleon recognized the important influence of the bar in the preservation of order and the administration of justice, and in his first consulate began a comprehensive code of laws and the education and elevation of the advocate. He called to his assistance the learning and the law of Portalis, Simeon, Fouchet and others and established schools of law at Paris and in the provinces, restored the roll of advocates and recognized its administration upon a firm and comprehensive basis. It is true that the larger liberty and greater influence they had exercised did not suit the ambitious and despotic emperor. The signal brilliancy and success with which Moreau and others, whom he would have crushed, were defended, taught him that freedom of speech and an independent advocacy were incompatible with despotism, and the liberties of the bar were greatly restricted. But the general plan of organi zation and education, then revived and adopted, have con tinued with constant improvement to the present time. With out enumerating the dates and details of the various amend ments and improvements, we will give a short account of this perfected organization. The theory that the advocate is an officer of the court and thus an officer of the government was carried to its logical and legitimate conclusion by provision by ordinances for the education, the organization and the control of the order.

### THE UNIVERSITY OF FRANCE

was created in 1806. Faculties were established for the various branches of learning, and especial care was taken in the organization of the faculties of law. The necessity for these faculties and the schools of law was ably presented

by M. Foucroy, Councillor of State, on recommending their
establishment to the Legislative Assembly. "It will," says
he, "drive away from the temple of the law those who would
dare profane it without a title and without knowledge; it
will form enlightened men for the profession of the bar; it
will contribute by good and competent studies to the re
appearance of those magistrates celebrated for their merits
and their virtue which have illustrated the two last centuries."
Terms of novitiation, of study, and examinations for licentia-
tion were prescribed. The curriculum provided embraced in
its comprehensive sweep the whole range of French and
Roman law—in strong contrast to that of the American
schools, with their few and short terms, meager list of
studies, loose examinations and ready diplomas. Mills of
the pigmies that grind exceedingly fast. Having passed the
terms and examinations, the student became the licentiate,
and subject to the control of the order, but before being
admitted to practice he still had to pass his "stage," above
referred to, of three or five years, to see if he was worthy
of being admitted to the roll of advocates. Each judicial
department has its roll of advocates, and each roll its batonier,
or president, and other officers, and also its council, whose
functions were the most important of the order. This
council has administrative, judicial and disciplinary at-
tributes; it admits or rejects; it tries all infractions of the
rules and ethics of the order, and censures, suspends or dis-
misses the guilty; it takes the licentiate by the hand and
directs his education and admission, and its care extends
even to the proper and appropriate ceremonies of his funeral
obsequies, and

### ENDS ONLY WITH THE GRAVE.

The order of advocates is controlled by a written code of
ethics, over fifty in number, deduced from the experience
of ages and embodying the best of those rules before adopted,
including some hereinbefore referred to. They embrace
every relation of the advocate, his general duties, his duty to
his clients, to his brother associates and toward the judges.
The first of these declares that one cannot be a perfect
advocate if he be not a good and honest man. They inculcate

diligence, sobriety, truth, honesty, courtesy, dignity and independence. They regulate by the highest standard the conduct of the advocate in every phase of his professional life. Nothing too small for its care, nothing too great for its control.

While it enjoins upon the advocate respect for and obedience to the court, it likewise demands the courtesy of the court to the bar, Rule 43 prescribes that the judge shall not interrupt the advocate while pleading. They are the best judges of the means to be employed in their client's causes. These are some, and but an example of this admirable code of ethics.

### THE BAR OF FRANCE,

then, is a thoroughly trained, educated and organized body. Educated in every department of learning, trained in the highest school of professional ethics, and organized to the encouragement and advancement of everything advantageous, and to the resistance of everything hurtful to their order or the State, the result was, in this modern as in the ancient bar, a succession of brilliant advocates, profound jurists. De-Toequeville and Von Holst both noticed the great preponderance of lawyers filling the highest offices in America. It is equally noticeable in France. A majority of the statesmen and ministers, and the most brilliant and effective of her orators in her Legislatures were lawyers. It is noticeable that, taking the batoniers of the order from 1836 to 1864, we find among them four Ministers of Justice, four of the Interior, two of Public Works, one of Foreign Affairs, one of Agriculture and Commerce, and one Vice-President of the Senate. We cannot pretend to notice or even enumerate the great lawyers of this century. We find, too, that their

### DISCIPLINE AND ORGANIZATION

gave them a power in the State. From Guizot to Draper their power and influence are recognized. They were the most persistent and dangerous enemy of aristocracy. They were the first to resist papal aggression and come to the assistance of Philip against Boniface. They overthrew superstition and magic, and replaced supernatural logic by philosophic logic. They resisted the ordinances of Blofs, first by a protest, and then in a body laying down their functions. They built the first barricades in Paris, and when Cardinal Mazarin exiled one of their number, Omer Talon, the whole bar again resigned and refused to plead until Talon was restored. In the Constituent Assembly Thouvet, Bornave and Chapelier were advocates, and Buzot, Vergniaud and Guadet were found in the Convention. The revolution of 1830 was called a revolution of advocates. This hasty sketch must be supplemented by something of the

### HABITS OF THE FRENCH BAR.

In the early period of French law, the ecclesiastical courts and the clergy administered the law. It was, hence, but natural that the courts and lawyers should have afterward retained the habits, customs and manners of those early tribunals. Oral pleadings for a long time resembled a sermon. A speech began with a text, selected generally from the Scriptures. This text then formed the initial sentence of each division and subdivision of the discourse, and repeated as often as, "He played upon the harp of a thousand strings." It was divided into numerous divisions and subdivisions, though not always after the rules of Locke or Quintillian, and interspersed with numerous anecdotes, wise saws and strange instances and with quotations from every source—Biblical, mythological, prose and poetry, Latin, Greek and Law-French—until the whole resembled a patchwork quilt, and reminded one of what Tickler, in Noctes, said of some one, "He had been at a great feast of languages and stolen the scraps." The scrap-book of quotations and citations from all authors, ancient and modern, profane and religious, was the lawyers' *vade mecum*. But it is doubtful if they also adopted the sing-song monotones of the clergy, as we find an early recommendation to them, after the advice of Hamlet to the players, that they should not gesticulate wildly with their head, hands or feet, nor display a great pomp in small cases, but that their voices and manner should be in harmony with the subject. They were also early enjoined to leave off all digression and go directly to the subject, and especially to leave off when done.

### THE CUSTOM OF ATHENS

should have been adopted. There the judges, in order to regulate the speeches of advocates, limited each party to the time it would take a certain quantity of water to run through a clepsydra, or kind of hour-glass. And when the water was out the lawyer had to quit. This is doubtless the origin of the modern slang, "Dry up." It is also related that a Roman advocate, whose name we cannot recall, whose habit was to speak too loud, corrected this by having a servant stand by and play upon a musical instrument, by the tones of which the speaker regulated his voice. Mark Twain once recommended a candidate for literary fame inquiring for the best brain food, that he should eat a couple of whales. Upon the same principle we would recommend to some members of the bar, we wot of, the Thomas orchestra or a national salute as modulator.

### PASQUIER, A TRULY GREAT LAWYER

and classic scholar, first discarded the text and quotation, and framed his style after the style of the best ancient writers and speakers. The innovation once begun soon spread until for style and manner the speeches of the French advocate became models of forensic eloquence. Whether the provincial advocate rode the circuit we are not informed. We find, however, advocates of one parliament appearing before other parliaments. And we can well imagine that they mounted their horses, with hat and gown in saddlebags, and jogged the circuit as did their brothers across the channel. And we dare say their horses, like Mr. Scott (Lord Eldon), often "demurred when they should have gone to the country." That they had the pernicious custom we have of signing petitions without care is certain. Gatray, an able but jocular advocate, caused nearly the entire bar of Paris to sign a petition to the Minister of Police regarding, as he said, a monopoly complained of by the town of Le Mons. The petition was presented and turned out to be a pasquinade of twenty-four pages entitled, Questions of State for the Fat Pullets of La Flesche Against Those of Le Mons, full of the most incredible absurdness and narrated in a style of pompous burlesque, Cicero, Cæsar, Thesus, Achilles, Homer and

Voltaire were quoted, The ridicule of the signers was complete.

Another instance is given of the Bar signing an elaborate petition to the Town Council to put a roof on the Town sun dial.

### THE FRENCH LAWYER

is, or should be, a more entertaining speaker, and the French magistrate a better judge than English or American, because he does not rely upon precedent, but reasons out each case by the fixed and unalterable rules of Justice and the elementary principles of the law. Sir Jonah Barrington, in his sketch of his own times and of Irish Bar, gives one of the reasons the Irish Judges search for, and rely upon precedents was, "because of their inability of the adoptors to make any better precedents themselves." De Tocqueville's Comment upon the American lawyer was that of surprise, "how often he quoted the opinion of others, how little he alludes to his own." The surprise would be greater now, when these borrowed opinions, these old clothes of dead cases, amounting now to over 40,000 volumes, have become the reliance of bench and bar; and this surprise would ripen to ridicule at the spectacle of a modern peripatetic court attempting, with the assistance only of the lawyers' briefs, to fit these old clothes to new subjects, differing as cases do differ with kaleidoscopic variation of fact; a spectacle as ludicrous as that of Fortuna putting the noses of some of her subjects on the faces of others. One, wearied with the vain search for truth through all these digests and cases, would gladly welcome a new Theophilus to give all this rubbish to the torch; and permit us to again become reasoning creatures instead of chronic case-hunters and case lawyers.

### WE BEG TO CONCLUDE

now with the practical applications of some few of the lessons forced upon us by this view of one of the most ancient, the most enlightened and most illustrious orders of advocates. This is the higher purpose of this paper to which we alluded in the opening. The first and highest lesson is union and organization. From these we may hope all the balance, for these will give the power for their attainment. The individual influence of the lawyer is felt in Church and State, in the marts of trade and the march of growth, but being individual is not fully recognized or accredited, nor fully felt. The voice of the bar is now the pipings of a single note, not the mutterings of universal thunder. It is the rout step of the army which breaks no bridges. In this day of the aggregation of capital and the combination of force, the capital and forces of the lawyer must be aggregated, else they will fall far below their former high estate. Already many evils have crept into the State, and in every department of the origination, the interpretation and the administration of the law, and in the morals and ethics of the bar. The people have left you the institution and organization by the Legislature of proper courts for the cheap and speedy administration of justice, and vet the "law's delay" is still a byword and a reproach. The people have tried waiting for you to catch up with the times, and taken the administration of justice in their own hands, and organized among themselves boards of arbitration for every chamber of commerce and every guild of trade. Laws depreciating the labor, the dignity and the worth of the judge have been passed, filling many benches with unlearned and incompetent incumbents.

### ADMISSION TO THE BAR

has become so easy of attainment that it is not appreciated, and offers no guarantee for the privileges it pretends to bestow. All these and many more evils should and can be corrected by first organizing the whole body of lawyers in one guild or corporation, first State and then National, and then proceed to enforce legislative legitimation, and thence to the regulation under statutes of its own order, and the enforcement of its own ordinances. The more thorough education and training of the law student must also take place. With the first century and era of our republic have passed the conditions of society and of American life which permitted, at the bar, in the pulpit, and in legislation, the uneducated, but strong, self-made men. The pioneer age is past, a new era has dawned, the man or lawyer of simple,

uneducated force must now give way to the profound jurist;
the scholar and the publicist. From this time forward there
must be a recognition of a new order of things, a new state
of society, a higher order of statesmanship, and a deeper
scholarship; and that profession which does not recognize
these facts will soon find itself behind the age, left, a land-
mark of time, and

### FIT SUBJECTS FOR THE FINGER OF SCORN.

Let us, therefore, take these matters into consideration
and vigorously proceed to the reorganization, the rehabilitation and the elevation of our order. And these State and
National bar associations must complete this work already
begun by them. It is in and by them the labor must be done.
Already much has been accomplished since their organization,
but more remains to be done. They should enlarge the scope
of their efforts to the embracement of everything regulating
the education, the admissions and the conduct of members
of the bar and pertaining to the administration of the law
It is only by this that the bar shall assert and maintain its
proud supremacy and be worthy the immortal encomium of
d'Agessau, "that the order of advocates is as noble as virtue."

# THE BEAUTIFUL

An Address delivered by the Hon. L. B. McFarland,
of Memphis, to the Alumnæ of the Clarksville Female
Academy, June, 1879.

(Those who heard this classical composition will be
pleased at seeing it in print. For their gratification and our
own we have prevailed upon the gifted orator to permit its
publication in our columns.)—Clarksville Chronicle. July 5,
1879.

### ADDRESS.

It was with much hesitancy we accepted the invitation
to be with you today. We were mindful that our audience
would be composed of men and women of learning and
culture, "scholars rich and ripe," and, above all, "sweet girl
graduates," as Tennyson calls them—the most critical and
merciless of hearers, fresh from those classic shades from
which the most arduous of professions has for years exiled
us: Enough to make us pause.

But then we wanted to come to Clarksville; we wished
to renew associations of camp and college that were pleasantly
remembered. The same promptings that brought so many
of the Alumnæ of this institute to this reunion brought us,
and our inclinations triumphed over our judgment and
prudence. We are here, like Labienus

Hopeless of pleasing, yet inclined to please.

Having determined to come, the next step was to
determine what subject would be appropriate to the time,
the place and the occasion. In this connection we remembered that Clarksville was the loveliest of places; that its ·hills
and its valleys, with their adornments of art and evidence of
taste, with the grand sweep of its majestic river, made it the
home of the beautiful; that we were to be surrounded by
beautiful women, and at a season of the year when the sunshine is sweetest and the flowers most lovely, and it occurred

to us that to talk of "The Beautiful" itself would not be inappropriate.

We will not undertake to define in what the beautiful consists, for its best exponent, Ruskin, has said that "it does not know that it is, or what it is," and Cousin has said that "the domain of beauty is more extensive than the physical world exposed to our view; it has no bounds but those of entire nature and of the soul and genius of man." We can only select select some of the most reasonable, and, to us, plausible theories of its exponents, and passing with hasty review from these, proceed to their practical application to the higher purposes of this address.

The beautiful—*to kalon*—was a favorite subject among the ancients, Plato and Aristotle being among the earliest writers, and it was not until the eighteenth century that investigation into the nature of the beautiful was brought again into the study of philosophy. Baumgarten made it a science, and that science he expressed by the word "aesthetics," from the Greek *"aesthanomai," I feel;* conveying the double idea of the effect of something without upon the something within.

Kant and Schelling and Schiller among the Germans, with Hutchinson and Jeffrey, Burke, Sir Joshua Reynolds, Allison and lastly, Ruskin among the British, with Cousin, of the French, have all written more or less upon science. Pericles in one of his letters to Aspasia, says, "The perfection of beauty is what is farthest from all similitudes to the brutes." It is useless, however, to attempt an analysis or comparison of the various theories of these, of which we might say almost generally, as was said of one, that "this was a rapturous Platonic doctrine, impossible to criticise because unintelligible." No definition has been able to express its effect. That certain physical objects are beautiful is admitted by all, and certain rules are established determining whether they are beautiful or not; but how these forms and combinations and colors impress man and give him the pleasurable sensibility of the beautiful is the vexed question. The aesthetic sense is the most difficult of interpretation in psychology. The child hovering above the flower in which trembles the dew drop—itself a human flower with its soul for a dew-drop; the lover, looking from the stars into the deeper heaven of his loved one's eyes; the artist who, like Vernet, lashed to the mast that he might view the storm, beholds its loveliness and sublimity; the virgin votary who bows before the altar while a wealth of harmony sweeps over her soul—each and all of these murmurs beautiful, beautiful, and yet they know not whence nor how comes this melody to their soul. We would say that the Beautiful is something mysterious and inexplicable, but a something that makes you bow the head in worship and sing—"Praise God from whom all blessings flow."

The simplest treatment of the subject divides it into *physical, intellectual* and *moral* beauty. This is Cousin, while Ruskin divides it into typical and vital beauty. We adopt the first, but both are but different forms of Schlegel, who analyzes the being of art and nature from the idea of beauty. The sound or sight, that is the object or being of beauty, and the sense or idea of beauty within ourselves.

Physical beauty is dependent upon order, harmony, proportion, sound, colors and movements. All the beauties of nature, whether the "wee crimson-tipped flower" or the majestic mountain, owe their effect to these. You examine the simplest object of art—a vase or painting—it has one kind of beauty. You turn from this and stand upon the mountain top and gaze into the far distance, over hill and valley, over stream and wood, and beyond still to the evening clouds which rest upon the far confines of the world—you see the sun sinking to rest, and "feel your heart float softly with him behind yon western paradise of clouds," until your soul expands and you drink in the magic beauty of the scene. This is another and different expression of beauty, differing in form, alike in result, but each springing from some combination of these elements—form, proportion, color, harmony.

What variety, what proportion, what unity in nature! 'Tis only the poet's pen, "trembling towards the inner founts of feeling," that can describe these beauties. How charmingly Milton pictures the quiet beauty of a day in Eden:

*"Sweet is the breath of morn, her rising sweet*
*With charm of earliest birds; pleasant the sun*
*When first on this delightful land he spreads*
*His orient beams on herb, tree, fruit and flower*
*Glistening with dew; fragrant the fertile earth*
*After soft showers, and sweet the coming on*
*Of grateful evening mild; then silent night*
*   *   *   and her fair moon,*
*And all the gems of heaven, her starry train."*

Lord Dunsany asks: "What is it to dislike poetry? It is to have no little dreams and fancies, no holy memories of golden days, to be unmoved by serene midsummer evenings or dawn over wild lands, singing or sunshine, little tales told by the fire a long time since, glow-worms and briar rose; for of all these things and more is poetry made. It is to be cut off forever from the fellowship of great men that are gone; to see men without their halos and the world without its glory; to miss the meaning lurking behind common things, like elves hiding in flowers; it is to beat one's hands all day against the gates of fairyland and to find that they are shut and the country empty and its king gone hence."

The love of nature is especially strong in youth. It is then, says Ruskin, "we have the most intense, superstitious, insatiable and beatific perception of her splendors." As we grow older this natural fondness for nature grows weaker, and our sensibility to its charms becomes dulled, because we fail to cultivate them and because human ties and selfish interests take their place. By cultivation these sensibilities can be quickened and kept alive. We can enjoy her beauties continually, and the landscape will be lovely whether we are looking forward in youth or backward upon it in age.

From physical we ascend to intellectual beauty, which comprehends everything commonly attributable to intellectual effort and included among the arts. The arts are in turn divided into two classes, those addressed to hearing—music and poetry, and those addressed to sight—painting, engraving, sculpture, architecture and, by some, landscape gardening is included. These are called the fine arts, as contra-distinguished from the useful, because they produce the disinterested emotion of beauty without regard to utility.

The sole object of art is the beautiful, and the art of poesy is but the language of that finer sensibility which *recognizes* the beautiful. It is difficult to classify music. As the end of art is the expression of moral beauty by the aid of physical beauty, music would seem to be the best exponent of art. It is in the expression of grief and sympathy music attains its highest power, touches the tenderest chords of the human heart. Nature's sweetest music is the *miserere* of the pines, or the low moaning of the night wind as it comes from the wrecks of the sea. What is comparable to the requiem of Mozart, or the miserere of Allegri? It is only in the deep pathos of such songs as the Three Fishers of Kingsley that poetry and music, sweet sisters of sorrow, thrill the human soul with divinest melody:

> *For men must work and women must weep,*
> *And the sooner it's over, the sooner to sleep,*
> *And good-bye to the bar and its moaning.*

As often as you have heard this song, and as old as it is, did you ever think of its deep, deep truth—

> *For men must work and women must weep,*

and its sad, sad wail of humanity—

> *And the sooner it's over, the sooner to sleep.*

"The sweetest songs are those that tell of saddest truth." It is an eastern saying that the nightingales of sweetest song are those whose nests are found nearest the tomb of Orpheus.

From intellectual we ascend to moral beauty, the glory and the grace and the light of the soul. It embraces justice, charity, truth and love. From beautiful things we rise to beautiful thoughts, and thence still higher to beautiful actions. Sculpture has sometimes been called frozen music; a beautiful action is the sculptured figure of a beautiful thought; it is the frozen music of a sweet soul; it leads to the infinite; it links man with God, the infinite type, the boundless expression of moral beauty. The doer of a good action is the greatest of artists, because without painter's brush or sculptor's chisel he or she expresses the highest type of the beautiful. In the cultivation of moral beauty we put in active exercise all the best forms of social and political ethics. We beautify the home and by charity abroad pour oil upon the troubled spirit, and bring balm to the bruised heart, and as we bind society together in the bonds of charity and love we strengthen the state. It is the healthful exercise of that within us which is immortal, and it is the effect of outward beauty upon this inner sensibility, of the finite upon the infinite, that gives us the highest appreciation of the beautiful. It is the suggestion of the infinite to the immortal that makes *distance* lend enchantment to the view, and makes the sunset and the hush of darkening evening twilight sink so deep into the soul, and creates within us that infinite longing, that *"sutzen pein"*—sweet pain—which is the highest effect of beauty.

It is not the hush of evening nor the sinking of twilight into shade that produces this. Says some one, "It matters little whether the bright cloud be little or manifold, whether the mountain line be subdued or majestic. It is not by the nobler form, it is not by the positiveness of hue, it is not by the intensity of light that this strange distant space possesses its attractive power. But there is one thing that it has, or suggests, which no other object or sight suggests, and that is *"infinity."*

It was a kind Providence that, having planted within us an immortal spirit, gave us the sky, an infinite expanse, in which to gaze and dream and gratify the love of the infinite. It is the play-ground of the soul. Artists soon learned this and saw the necessity of giving some glimpse of the beyond to each picture—some suggestion of the infinite. If a scene within doors, then, an open window or balcony; if landscape, however dense the shade, a little rift through which the open sky and infinite space may be seen; and modern art, even to photography, prefers its subjects so that beside or beyond them may be a glimpse of sky or ocean.

But the higher purposes of this address, and its practical application to which we referred in the beginning, were to insist that woman is the highest type of the beautiful, and the cultivation of woman the highest aim of humanity.

In all the various modes by which man expresses his idea of the beautiful, whether in poetry or song, in painting or sculpture, the highest attainment and most perfect execution has been in giving shape and form and character to lovely woman. The highest attainment of artistic beauty was in Greek art, and then not until Greek artists took woman as their model and the very highest type of the beautiful. As in architecture the first half of the Grecian age embodied strength and solidity, and the second half elegance and delicacy; so in sculpture and painting the first half illustrated the placid majesty of the gods, while the second half represented the grace and beauty of the goddesses. It was then woman became the Corinthian wreath to the temple of beauty. It was not until Aphrodite, redolent with spontaneous charms, landed upon the blossoming shores of Paphos and was reproduced in the Venus de Medici, and of Milo and many others; it was not until the people of Croton gathered the fairest of its daughters before Zeuxis in order that from their varied charms he might combine all in his masterpiece of Helen, that woman became the real type, and beauty the characteristic of Grecian art. Then Egypt, Persia and all the Peloponesus lent to Athens all that which was grand in conception, noble in design and perfect in execution. Beauty adorned the Acropolis and the Parthenon, lived in the statues of Scopas and Phidias, glowed in the canvas of Apelles and Pharrasius, breathed in the oratory of Aeschines and Demosthenes and sparkled in the poetry of Anacreon and Pindar.

In every age and with every nation art has attained its greatest perfection and approached nearest the ideal in illustrating the perfect beauty of perfect woman.

What would poetry be without woman?—and mind we are not speaking alone of physical beauty, for it is a significant fact, noticed by an accurate writer, that the graces of intellect and the charm of manner are no less remarkable in Asapasia and Cleopatra than the beauty of their persons. Shakespeare has scarcely a hero; he has only heroines.

It is only recently we heard a distinguished lecturer comment upon the fact that it was not until the pure pen of woman and the impress of her character came to English literature that it became potent to cultivate and refine a people. Who can measure the influence for good of the pens of Mrs. Norton, Mrs. Hemans, and above all and beyond all, and nearer and dearer than them all, Mrs. Browning.

As woman is the highest type of the beautiful, so the highest type of woman is she who combines within herself in the greatest perfection the essential elements of beauty—physical, intellectual and moral. It is in the cultivation of the intellect, the elevation of the soul, that woman approaches nearest the perfect type of beauty, and she fulfills her highest mission in cultivating the beautiful in herself and others. She must herself attain to an accurate sense of the beautiful by earnest, loving and unselfish attention to her impressions of it, not to the neglect of other aims and other duties, but by humble and loving ways to make herself susceptible to deep delight from the meanest objects of creation, and feel that

> "There's beauty all around our paths, if but
>     our watchful eyes
> Can trace it midst familiar things and
>     through their lowly guise."

She must see beauty in nature and art, the meanest rill, the mightiest river, in the pebble upon the shore and the great sea itself, "and music in its roar," and then ascending higher to the beautiful of music and poetry, and still ascending yet to a still loftier height, to *charity* and *duty* and *love*.

Goethe said "the two most beautiful things in all the world were the bright sky above us and the sense of duty within our hearts." Plato prescribed to artists that they should create nothing illiberal or deformed, but should cultivate only the beautiful—words that should be engraven in every home and seminary, and in the memory and heart of every girl and woman. There never was a time in the history of any people more favorable to the cultivation of the arts and the advancement of every aesthetic taste than the present in

America. Mr. Buckle says a people must first become wealthy before they can become learned; that while engaged in the mere struggle for subsistence no very deep learning can be attained. This is partially true, but the majority of the people of our country are now in that condition that much time cannot be given to education and to the cultivation of the arts. They have passed the pioneer age, passed the age of mere struggle for subsistence and come now to the age of adornment and the cultivation of the beautiful. Art galleries such as the Corcoran at Washington, and the National Academy of Design, and art journals like Appleton's are rapidly spreading abroad a love of the beautiful, refining the taste and elevating the morals of the people. The stately halls of the Hudson, and the lovely homes of the Schuylkill and Potomac equal, in taste the stately homes of England, the sweet villas by the Rhine. Our artists like Hosmer, Powers, Vinnie Ream, Beard and Hart are bringing us to the days of true Athenian glory, while our poets, Longfellow, Bryant, Ryan and Poe, though some dead, are singing to the world. Here is the true sphere of woman, and in this revival of the arts, and this quickened activity in the cultivation of the beautiful is her glorious opportunity for the achievement of that high place to which she was destined. It is a solemn duty to bring every sense into that state of cultivation in which it shall form the truest conclusions and attain the highest pleasure. Ignorance is never bliss. Think you the unlettered boor, the illiterate Gurth, perpetual thrall of Cedric ignorance—who treads the daisy beneath his feet, who walks through leafy shades and upon grand mountains, and yet sees no beauty in any of these—enjoys the happiness of that man or woman whose taste is cultivated, whose sensibilities quickened, beholds the beauty of one, the glory of the other.

That is the best mother who, herself seeing and feeling, teaches her child to note the beauty of earth and sky, of the cloud and the rainbow, the stars and the dew on the grass; every flower that she plants, every vine that she trails, every picture she paints, and everything of beauty with which she surrounds her home and family, every poem or song she teaches her children, every beautiful thought she quickens in their mind or high sentiment of duty and love she instills into their soul, but increases their capacity for enjoyment and ensures to them the greater happiness. And it is by beautifying herself, body, mind and soul, that she surrounds herself with an atmosphere delightful to men. The cultivation of the beautiful, appealing as it does to the aesthetic sense of man, is her true power. It is thus the willing captive throws her charms around the barbarous captor and subjects him to a vassalage infinitely more glorious than all his boasted majesty and power. It is thus the beautiful Parthenia, wreathing flowers about the cup, tames the barbarous Ingomar and leads him to paths of pleasantness and peace and deeds of higher glory.

The perfect woman is she who heightens the charms of her person by obedience to the laws of health and the suggestions of cultivated taste, who wields the full power of dress and the coquetry of ribbons, who weaves her tresses into raven and golden meshes to entrap the hearts of men, is she who cultivates her mind, fits herself for his companionship, and, above all, she who, elevating and illuminating her soul by deeds of sweet charity and divine love, lifts mortals to the skies. Such must have been the wife of Sir Thomas Lucy, for at Stratford-upon-Avon, in Charlecote Church, reads the epitaph with which the old knight himself commemorated his wife, "All the time of her life a true and faithful servant of her good God; never detected of any crime or vice; in religion most sound; in love to her husband most faithful and true; in friendship most constant; to what in trust was committed to her, most secret; in wisdom excelling; in governing her house and bringing up of youth in the fear of God that did converse with her, most rare and singular; a great mountain of hospitality; greatly esteemed of her betters; misliked of none, unless of the envious. When all is spoken that can be said, a woman so furnished and garnished with virtue as not to be bettered and hardly to be equaled of any. As she lived most virtuously, so she died most godly. Set down by him that did best know what hath been written to be true." With such women as contemporaries, no wonder that Shakespeare could scarce write a play without a perfect woman.

Trotters

## ELLEMAC STOCK FARM.

FOURTH OF JULY, 1892, AT ELLEMAC, CELEBRATED BY A GRAND BARBECUE
IN OLD STYLE. SOME ACCOUNT OF THE DAY AND ITS PLEASURES.
(*Memphis Appeal*, July 5, 1892.)

Yesterday while all Memphis was proclaiming its joy at the one hundred and sixteenth anniversary of the nation's birth in a manner so dear to the heart of the small boy, the day was being celebrated at Ellemac with a royal barbecue given by its hospitable owner in honor of a score or more of chosen friends.

Invitations had been issued for 50 guests, but the low-lying clouds and generally threatening aspect of the weather caused many to remain at home. Nevertheless there was a fair sprinkling of teams as early as 7 o'clock on the Horn Lake road, all traveling in the same direction, among them being a number of Memphis' most speedy roadsters, driven by their owners.

Ellemac Stock Farm is the pride of West Tennessee. Situated on an elevated plain eight miles from the City of Memphis, on the beautiful gravel road leading to Horn Lake, in the midst of one of the prettiest sections of country in the Sunny South, in the center, too, of a cotton growing community, it stands out in bold and beautiful contrast with the farms surrounding it. Judge L. B. McFarland, the proprietor, began this enterprise about six years ago by buying up an aggregate of 1,700 acres of old fields dotted over with the usual amount of gaping washes, grown up in bushes, and bearing every other token of long neglect and unskilled tillage. He began by enclosing the whole tract in neat and substantial plank and wire fences; then teams and scrapers were put to work: the gullies were filled in and leveled, and protected by circling and terracing. The whole was then divided into eighty acre lots, with a main lane or road running east and west the whole length of the farm, straight through the center. These lots were sown at first in peas and afterwards in clover, and still later in clover with a mixture of from three to five of the leading meadow grasses. The result is a lot of beautiful substantial meadows and some as fine farming lands as can be found in this section of country. Thirty-two bushels of oats and one and a half to two tons of hay per acre was harvested last year on land that, five years ago, with difficulty grew cow peas. In due time substantial and becoming barns, toolhouses, graineries, stables, cowhouses and tenant-houses were erected, a permanent, deep, clean pond of water made in each lot, and the place stocked with Southdown sheep, Ayrshire and Hereford cattle, a lot of fine, well-bred individual mares, and the improvements increased as fast as necessity demanded. There is at present not less than forty to fifty miles of substantial plank and wire fences. The outhouses, counting toolhouse for the farm machinery, stables and barns, comprise eight large and ornamental buildings. Everything in the way of live stock is well housed, from the big drove of diminutive Shetland ponies up to the four fine thoroughbred stallions.

Yesterday as the visitors drove up the avenue, shaded with a double row of apple trees, toward the house, the view that unfolded itself, as it were, around them, was most picturesque. On the left, set in a grove of magnificent oaks, up to whose mighty trunks, the lush grass grew rich and close, stood the hospitable home of the owner. Back of this clustered the barns and stables, and the buildings of the servants, while around and beyond all lay broad fields of 40 and 80 acres, verdant with clover, orchard grass, red-top and bermuda as juicy and succulent as was ever cropped by even that queen of the turf, Maud S. herself. But Ellemac does not consist entirely of grass lands, as the dark green of the growing corn and the golden yellow of the ripened oats plainly tell.

The manager of the farm, Mr. W. R. Tomlinson, lives there with his wife and family, at the Lower Farm, as it is called, which is a mile or thereabouts from the Upper Farm. Into his hands is trusted the task of keeping up the fields, and that he knows his business, their present condition shows.

The stable on the Upper Farm, where the "standards" are quartered, was naturally the point of greatest interest to the guests. It is a cleanly, commodious structure, with a large loft above, and divided below into 10 box stalls that open on two opposite sides, thus affording every opportunity for removing the stock in case of fire. A harness room, and an office, where the books and pedigrees of the horses are kept, are among the conveniences of the building, and a neat trough kept constantly filled with pure fresh water by means of a force pump, was also noted.

Of the horses themselves French Plate, the great stallion, Filoselle, the filly and Ellemac the beautiful 2-year-old, were the most interesting.

French Plate (registered 13,078) is seal brown in color, star and snip and white hind foot, and was four years old in April, 1892. He is, as his breeding indicates, a patrician in appearance and fact, strong and of great substance with no evidence of coarseness. His body is full, well rounded and placed upon the kind of legs that carried his famous old sire, Wedgewood, through so many well-earned victories. A glance at his pedigree shows a combination of the blood of Rysdyk's Hambletonian, Mambrino Chief and Pilot, Jr., the three trotting families that have furnished our greatest performers. The paternal line traces through Wedgewood, 2:19, the greatest campaigner of his day, to Belmont, sire of Nutwood, 2:18¾, thence through Abdallah, 15, sire of the incomparable Goldsmith Maid, 2:14, to Hambletonian, 10.

His dam, Mary B. 2:29, was sired by Alcaldric by Mambrino Chief.

Ellemac, the pride of the farm for which she is named, is a beautiful 2-year-old as ever nibbled a tuft of grass. She was bred on the farm by her present owner, and was foaled by Alvin, by Bostwick Almount, out of Fanny. Her dam was Linda. Though young Ellemac is 15½ hands 1½ inches high. She is bay in color, and so gentle that a child could drive her. From the tip of her dainty nose to the end of her silky tail, Ellemac gives evidence of her blood. The fine lines of her head, alert pointed ears, long neck, deep chest, short back and powerful flanks, all tell eloquently of speed and staying qualities. Everyone about the farm, from her trainer, Mr. D. J. Kearney, down to the lowliest stable boy, is her devoted slave and admirer. Yesterday, as she stood in her roomy stall, the cynosure of many critical eyes, she champed impatiently, as much annoyed as any regal beauty would be by the unusual intrusion, and even the words of praise that were bestowed upon her failed to smooth her ruffled feelings. Ellemac is a striking example of what may be accomplished in the way of breeding trotting horses on Shelby County soil, and her owner, inasmuch as she is the first he has bred, is very proud of her.

At 1 o'clock dinner was served on tables spread under the oaks. Everything on the menu, and the same was by no means of small variety, was grown on the farm. At the table were Messrs. W. B. Mallory, C. W. Metcalf, P. H. Bryson, N. C. Perkins, Jr., John Cuneo, W. L. Meux, Martin Mitchell, J. H. T. Martin, Ogden Fontaine, William Bowles, L. B. McFarland, U. W. Miller, Dick Hutton, Edward Fontaine, D. G. Kearney, Ed. Mhoon, R. Gill, G. Risley and Dr. F. Raines and Squire Stewart and others. The meal passed off very pleasantly, and Mr. and Mrs. Tomlinson were repeatedly congratulated on the success with which the barbecue was carried on. Under one of the trees a couple of kegs of beer and a demijohn of Lincoln County were on tap, and as their contents diminished the fun increased.

After dinner at each of these annual occasions our host selected one of the guests to read the Declaration of Independence, in patriotic celebration of the day. Then cigars with liquid accompaniment with anecdotes and jokes when all adjourned to the race track, excepting Mr. Mallory and J. H. T. Martin, who shouldered their guns and went off to the field near by for a couple of dead doves that Mr. Metcalf declared he either shot or scared to death in the morning. They didn't find them.

The race track, which is a fine half-mile course, was in bad condition, owing to the recent heavy rains, and was too deep in mud to attempt any speeding on, but half a dozen horses were brought out and trotted around the track on exhibition. The guests sat upon the fence and criticised the various horses as they appeared, all but Mr. Fontaine, who said he would rather take his chances in his buggy than risk his neck on the same fence with Farmer Levi.

It is the intention of Judge McFarland to demonstrate that standard horses can be successfully bred on Shelby County soil, and from the handsome beginning he has made, there seems to be no room to doubt that he will succeed. In the fields and paddocks of the farm are 15 handsome colts sired by the stallion French Plate, and it was a pretty sight to watch them grazing by the side of their dams, and one that is of itself well worth a drive out to Ellemac.

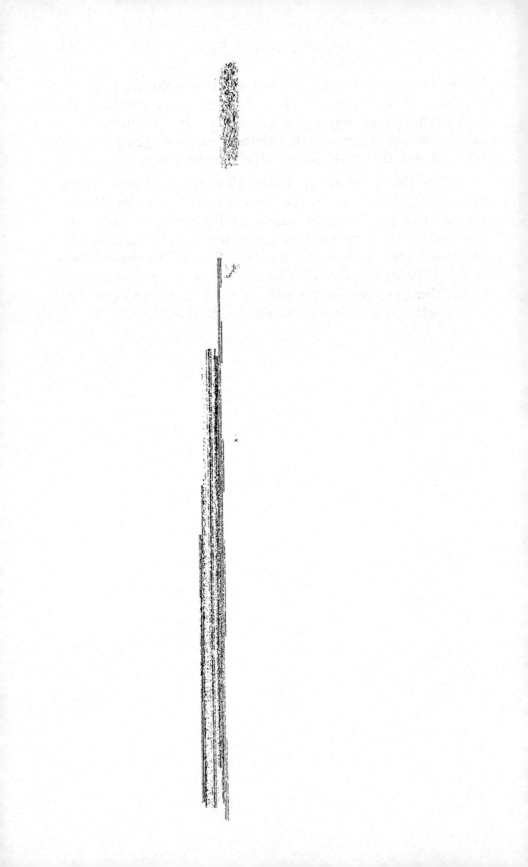

# TOAST TO THE LADIES.

### BAR ASSOCIATION OF TENNESSEE, 1889.

#### AT THE BANQUET

The Annual Banquet took place at the Fountain Head Hotel at 9 o'clock P. M., J. M. Dickinson presiding. Later Secretary of War, and Assistant Attorney General of U. S.

The following sentiments, among others, were offered:

"Our Outgoing President." Response by J. W. Judd.

"Our Incoming President." Response by H. H. Ingersoll.

"The Supreme Court of Tennessee." Response by D. L. Snodgrass.

"The State of Tennessee." Response by G. W. Pickle.

"Our Brethren who are Absent in Body, but are Present in Spirit." Response by Xen. Wheeler.

"Our Published Proceedings." Response by Jno. Ruhm.

"The Ladies." Response by L. B. McFarland.

"Vote Necessary to Carry Prohibition Amendment." Response by H. M. Wiltse.

"Our Country." Response by Tom Fort.

"The Days and the Ways of the Old Bar." Response by George Brown.

"The Docket Cleaners." Response by Josiah Patterson.

"The Senior Bar," Response by W. P. Washburn.

"The Junior Bar." Response by A. D. Marks.

Mr. McFarland said:

#### "THE LADIES."
##### Toast at Banquet, Tennessee Bar Association.
##### RESPONSE OF L. B. McFARLAND.

"Mr. Chairman—It is the perfection of cruelty to expect a lover of the perfection of humanity to do this subject

justice on an hour's notice.  On any notice I should feel
hesitancy in responding to this toast, knowing—

"I shall lack voice; the deeds of Coriolanus
Should not be utterly feebly,"

It is a theme that has interested the voice and pen of all
the most eloquent.  The inspiration of the poet and the
genius of the painter have sung and painted her beauties.
From Ariosto to Tennyson, from Correggio to Meissonier,
she has been the one universal theme and subject; and from
Rabelais and Burton to Mark Twain and the latest Puck, she
has been the fair mark for all shafts of wit.

In all this richness of material, memory will inevitably
volunteer her stores, and a speaker unwittingly use her contributions.

In one of Scott's novels, the Antiquary I think, the
preface suggests that much of the materials of the after-
story was taken from an old manuscript, and the author
adds:  "pray the reader if he finds anything especially prosy
or uninteresting in this story, he will credit it to the manuscript; if anything bright or beautiful, as from the author,"
—or words to that effect.

So I beg you gentlemen to attribute anything dull or
flat I may now say to Burton or Mark Twain; anything good
or witty to the speaker.

To begin at the beginning of the subject, I wish to say
most positively I do not concur in the modern Darwinian
theory of the origin of woman.

They, the exponents of this theory, assert that instead
of a woman being formed from the rib of a man, she was
made from the tail of the monkey—man.  They say that
since the appearance of woman, this caudal appendix to man
has disappeared.  They cite the antics women are sometimes
guilty of as a tendency to revert back to original instincts,
and argue from her clinging nature that this is also monkey
instinct.  They noted, clinging to trees—I call this merely
"monkeying" with the question.  You remember, speaking

of this clinging nature of women—often to worthless men, some one has beautifully likened her to the vine—that the worse the ruin, the closer she clings; and some would-be wit and actual wretch has added, "and the closer she clings the worse the ruin."

But all these false theories and false comparisons I distinctly repudiate. I hold to the ancient and honorable Biblical Genesis, that she was made of the rib of a man—taken from under his arm that he should shelter her, from near his heart that he should cherish and love her. Speaking of the creation, it is well enough to put in a word for old Adam occasionally. He has been much and unjustly abused about that apple-eating episode.

Now I suggest there is not a man at this table that would not have done the same thing with half the provocation. Suppose any of you—our President, for instance—found yourself some summer afternoon, mercury 100, in a garden that Shenstone would have enjoyed, lying upon a mossy bank, and lulled to rest and dreams of love by murmuring waters and the bulbul's song, while the spirit of fragrance from his harem of flowers made sweet the air. Suppose that in an hour like this there appeared to you the most beautiful woman in the world. Suppose she came to you in all the native loveliness of womanly perfection or I might now add, bathing costume, and, putting her arm around your neck, gave you an apple, and said, in the softest and most musically silvery of voices, "Eat, my love"; wouldn't you eat? Why, sir, you would eat an acre of crab apples.

From Eve on up woman has been the most tempting and the most charming of creatures.

Some one has said, "there is no living with her on account of her whims and caprices"; but adds, "there is no living without her on account of her charms."

Looking down the whole vista of human existence, what noble examples do we see? There's Cleopatra and Lucretia Borgia; there's Mrs. Macbeth; there's the Daughter of the

Regiment, and Susan B. Anthony. Who will live longer on the pages of history than these?

Whenever a poet, or a painter or a sculptor wanted to make something perfect, he took a woman for his model.

In sculpture, from the Minerva of Phidias, which looked down from the Parthenon, to the Greek Slave of Powers; and in painting, from the Iphigenia of Timanthes to the Madonnas of Raphael and Holbein; while in poetry, we have the early and perfect type of Helen, of whom

> "They cried, No wonder such artistic charms
> For seven long years have set the world in arms;
> What winning grace and what majestic mein.
> She moves a goddess, and she looks a queen."

If for nothing else, Shakespeare would be immortal in his female character. There is hardly a play in which there is not a perfect woman. Cordelia, steadfast in grave hope, high duty, and errorless purpose; Desdemona, Hermione, Virginia, Perdita, and Helen are all faultless, and Portia, "so much more elder than her looks."

So in Scott, from pure and lofty Ellen Douglass, to brave and gentle Jennie Dean. The Greek's heroines, from Andromache to patient Penelope, the Beatrice of Dante's great poem, are all ideal types of human faith, human love, and divinely human beauty.

She is, sir, a great success at everything she undertakes. No one can sew on a button or darn a sock as she. She throws a charm around the most grotesque of costumes. Who could wear a bustle or sport a pin-back but a woman? The Grecian bend becomes with her Hogarth's line of beauty, and a pyramid of hat the perfection of prettiness.

As an ice cream consumer she is without parallel. My heart goes out in pity and sympathy for the country youth who, having only a dollar, promises two girls ice cream. On reaching the saloon he is paralyzed with the placard on the window, "Ice Cream, $1.50 per *gal.*"

As a sweetheart she is, as one of our Supreme Court Reporters says, "without a peer and without an equal;" while as a wet nurse she is simply grand (I know that wet nurse is Twain's, I never had a wet nurse).

Without her the divine art of kissing would fade into innocuous desuetude.

She is the other self to man always.  Without her he is simply nobody.  There is an ancient fable that originally there was but one creature, combining all the characteristics of both sexes; but the gods, seeing these were greater than they, determined to divide and out of the man was made a woman.

Happy the man who has this "alter ego;" happy the lawyer who has his "Hannah Jane."

> "Had Lord Alfred found that rare communion
>     which links,
> What woman feels purely, what man nobly thinks,
> His shrewd tact had moulded and mastered at
>     length
> The world that now mastered and moulded his will."

Without her, what would man be?  A body without soul, a harp without strings, a lamp unlit.

She is the holiness of every relation of life.

EXTRACTS FROM

# BENCH AND BAR OF SHELBY COUNTY.

BY L. B. McFARLAND FOR

HISTORY OF MEMPHIS

BY J. M. KEATING.

### JUDGE ARCHIBALD WRIGHT.

JUDGE ARCHIBALD WRIGHT. Had a stranger been standing upon the corner of Main and Madison Streets late any afternoon a few years ago, he would have noticed there a group of persons. He would have noticed that the central figure of this group was an old man some seventy years of age, tall, though slightly bent, robust, rugged, with gray hair, keen gray eyes, prominent cheek, low forehead, and with a red bandana handkerchief which he alternated from one hand to his mouth and then to the other hand. His dress was of the age just after knee breeches had disappeared. A broad brimmed soft hat, broad open collar, pants of the old style, and large, comfortable shoes were the characteristics of his dress. This was Judge Archibald Wright, the Saul, the Nestor and the Cato of the Memphis bar. Archibald Wright was born in the County of Maury, Tenn., on the 29th of November, 1809, but was reared in Giles County; was educated at Mount Pleasant Academy and Giles College; read law with Judge Bramlett, and obtained license to practice in 1832. He was a volunteer and served a campaign in the Florida war. On the 29th of May, 1837, he married Miss Mary Elizabeth Eldridge. He removed to Memphis in 1851 and formed a partnership with T. J. Turley. In 1856, he was appointed a member of the Supreme Court of Tennessee and was elected to the same office in 1858, and remained upon the bench until the sound of arms stilled the voice of justice.

He was an ardent Southerner, and went with the south in the great contest, giving two sons to active service, he himself going with them and staying with the army, though not

as a soldier, until the war was ended. There was no better
known figure in the Army of Tennessee than that of Judge
Wright, mounted on a large gray mule, wearing his red
bandana *in his mouth* and always found near the thunder of
his son's battery. After the war he returned to Memphis and
practiced law here, in the Supreme Courts of adjoining States,
and at Washington. As a man, Judge Wright was a link between the past and the present; but was so firmly pressed and
fashioned in the first that it took  none of the characteristics
of the present. Though not himself a pioneer, he came of and
after them so shortly that all the best of their traits were his.
He retained all the simplicity, the directness and the honesty
of the manner and habit of this age. Severe in speech and
rugged in manner, it was still that severity which is simple
honesty, and that ruggedness which is the mere scorn of
fashion, and never vulgar or ill-bred. He had no fondness
for literature and read no books, but of law. He was never
known to make a quotation. His knowledge was unusually
practical. He had read men and events, however, never forgot
anything he had once learned; and had thus accumulated a
vast storehouse of useful knowledge, which he had at full
command, and drew from with ready hand. He had grown
up, as it were, with the state, with its legislative, political
and judicial history. He had read no books in all his life
perhaps on political economy, and knew  nothing  of  the
technical rules and scientific theories of government, but
had been familiar for half a century with the rise and progress
of the State and National government, and watched with a
keen appreciative intellect the suggestion, advancement and
fate of principles of government, had seen the rise and fall of
parties, and had thus become, by practical experience
thoroughly familiar with the spirit and genius of American
government and progress. He had grown up with the legislative history of Tennessee. Its statute laws were almost a
part of his own life and thought. He not only knew when
such and such statutory innovations were made, but knew the
circumstances which led up to such enactments, the reasons
therefor and the remedies that were intended. It was the
same as to all the earlier decisions of the Supreme Court. He

not only remembered the cases themselves and the principles decided, and how one modified or reversed the other, but also in many instances knew the parties themselves and remembered counsel employed, and their arguments in the particular cases. He was not contemporary of Reese, Green, McKinney, and Caruthers, and Marshall and Fogg and Ewing and many others of that bright galaxy that preceded the war. He had not the polished learning of Reese, the full reading of Green, the impetuous strength of McKinney, or the grace and fluency of Marshall and Ewing, and yet in all the solid attainments of the lawyer and the sturdy virtues of the man, he was the peer of them all. Like these, his reputation was not confined to any one section of the state, but belonged in common to all. He was perhaps the most careful, laborious and painstaking practitioner that was ever at this bar. His habit was where a case was submitted to him, to first make himself familiar with all the facts. He would then prepare an elaborate brief on the questions of law in the case, and then address himself to getting up in the most careful way, every particle of evidence attainable to make out his case. Then before it was called for hearing, he prepared himself 'for argument by the most exhaustive research. His pleading was elaborate, but his opponent always found on hearing that no amendments to Judge Wright's pleadings were needed for him to get in all of proof, authority and argument he wanted. In argument he took his time, and said all that could properly be said on his side, submitting every proposition that could possibly bear on the case. His pleadings, briefs and arguments as a lawyer were the very antipodes in style, of his opinions as a judge. The last were models of brevity, terseness and point. When asked to explain this he said in his curt way: "When I was deciding myself, I knew what I was going to decide; when before the court, I don't know what some fool judge may decide."

In argument he covered the table with books, and usually commenced with the earliest enunciation of the principle relied upon, and traced it through the English and American decisions to the present. He used no notes or written memoranda, but with memory of dates and cases as remarkable as that of Macaulay, referred in succession to sometimes twenty cases, giving from memory, style of case, with book, page and the reasonings of the court.

In practice, while he had nothing of the trickster or pettifogger, he recognized the truth of what a recent German writer had ably presented, "That every lawsuit was a war, and the forces engaged in hostility to each other," and woe to the opponent who came to the battle without full armor. Lord Coke says that "a great learned man is a long time in making." So of Judge Wright, as a lawyer. He was made a great lawyer by the years and the events through which he passed. He was the last, too, of such lawyers. The circumstances which surrounded his life and moulded and pressed his mind and character have passed forever. The days of pioneer simplicity are gone. The decisions and statutes are too numerous and voluminous for any one henceforth to follow and master them as they grow. The lawyer of principles must give way, to a great extent, to the lawyer of precedents.

The most assiduous student, the most active practitioner, the most earnest citizen cannot hope to grow up with and become a part of the law and history of his time, as did the subject of this sketch. There will never be another Archibald Wright.

"Are yet two Romans living, such as these?
The last of all the Romans, fare-thee-well."

Of his private virtues, did space permit, we could say much that was true and beautiful. These live in the hearts and worthy lives of his children, as his public merit is made perpetual in the archives of the state.

### GEORGE R. PHELAN.

In 1866 there came to Memphis from Mississippi, a young lawyer, George R. Phelan, who very soon became a conspicuous figure at the bar and in the politics of the state. He was the son of James Phelan, senator from Mississippi to the Confederate Congress and afterwards practicing law in Memphis.

George Phelan was tall, slender, erect, graceful and dignified. His mouth was delicate but firm, his chin square and strong, his eyes keen, gray and well apart, and above towered a high forehead, backed by a magnificent head that gave evidence of much breadth. His whole appearance was that of alertness and courage. He was in character the very embodiment of the aristocratic youth of the south. Quick to anger, slow to forgive, vindictive, haughty, imperious and jealous of honor, "as an eagle of her aerie," and yet withal, soft and gentle as a woman to those he loved. His talents were of the very highest order, his cultivation the very best. Not after the order of the schools, but after the bent of his own genius. He had followed the instincts of his own inclination and made himself. With an intense thirst for knowledge he had, alone and unaided, taken up and studied such subjects as were most pleasing to him. The sea and the science of war were his loves. He studied naval architecture and the charts of the sea, with its wind and water currents, with ardor. He studied the art of war and the science of tactics and strategy with an assiduity and thoroughness that made him one of the most finished and caustic critics of modern tactics. He published but little, but left many manuscripts of comment and criticism upon the campaigns of the war. Politics and political economy also engaged his attention, and he became familiar with its writings from Ricardo and Machiavelli to Henry George. Polite literature he devoured as a pastime, the law he studied as an instrument.

The affection of the writer for the subject prompts the most extended notice the limits of these pages will permit, but his life and character justify far more than the space claimed. His character was the most unique and his brief

career in Memphis the most conspicuous of any that has ever
belonged to its bar.   His life was a very romance of stirring
and dangerous adventure.   He was reared at Aberdeen,
Miss., and before he was twelve, and while other boys of his
age were playing marbles and ball, he was devouring Mayne
Reid's "Boy Hunters," "Cooper's Tales," "Arabian Nights"
and "Poe's Tales."   He read Waverly in twenty-seven con-
secutive heats, almost without pausing to take breath.   An
old friend tells of his establishing in the corner of the yard,
a wigwam made of an old blanket and some sticks, before
which he would sit for hours wrapped in another blanket and
holding an old musket, playing Indian chief.   At ten he rebelled against the authority of his father, headed a rebellion
and secession of several other boys and started down the
Tombigbee to the sea.   At fourteen he joined the Confederate
army and served for some months in Virginia until the term
of his enlistment was out.   He was then sent to the military
school at Tuscaloosa, from which he was expelled the first
session for general deviltry.   He then, without money, started
for Texas and Mexico on foot, made his way across the
Mississippi, his only companion a rifle, thence to Brownsville
and Matamoras and thence down the Rio Grande to the
mouth.   Here he met the captain of a schooner bound for
New Orleans and he engaged to work his passage.   He was
at first dreadfully sick.   "Such," he wrote afterwards, "was
my introduction to the ocean, and rough as it was, I love the
sea with an ardent passion."   The cook becoming sick, he
took his place at five dollars per month.   Arriving at New
Orleans he shipped on another schooner for Philadelphia, at
ten dollars per month.   He finally landed at New York,
ragged and with three dollars in money.   In order to get
south again he enlisted in the Fourteenth New York Cavalry,
Colonel Mott commanding.   Before the regiment left New
York, they were called to assist in quelling the celebrated
riot there and a few shots were fired and several killed.   His
regiment was finally sent around by an old hulk of a steamer
to New Orleans and thence to Opelousas, La., with the Confederates in front.   Here he seized the first opportunity of
picket duty and escaped to the Confederate lines.   He was
then sixteen years of age.

In December, 1863, he started on foot for Aberdeen and crossed the Mississippi at night under the shadow of a Federal gunboat. Arriving at Aberdeen, he soon tired there, and went to Richmond, Va. Here, his father being a senator, and his youthful exploits becoming known, he was soon the talk of the town and the lion of the hour. He again joined the Confederate army and served with distinguished gallantry until the end of the war. He then studied law assiduously for a year and came to Memphis in August, 1866. Success was slow at first and he lived very hard, sleeping, as he said, on the sofa in his office and eating where he could the cheapest. He went to New York on some business and while there fell in with prominent Fenians and engaged in an expedition to Ireland as colonel of cavalry. Finally reaching the coast of Ireland, he and another landed, and while he was ashore the ship and crew were captured, and a five hundred pound reward was offered for the capture of Colonel Phelan, which was read to him by one of the detectives then searching for him. He soon escaped to England, visited Mr. Benjamin, from whom he borrowed enough to pay his passage to New York, and came thence back to Memphis. He was then an experienced and full fledged Fenian and at once organized a large Fenian circle in Memphis. The Irish were from this time forth his ardent admirers, sworn supporters and steady constituents. Tiring of the monotony of Memphis and the law, in 1867 he went to Brazil to join its army. He was promised a colonelcy, but before his commission was given him he was out of money, and again shipped at Rio Janeiro for Demarara before the mast. Touching at Georgetown he headed a remonstrance of the crew against the captain and a row ensued. The captain drew his pistol to kill Phelan, but he coolly suggested to the captain that if he should accidentally miss, his dirk, which he always carried, "would lovingly seek his bowels." The captain took his suggestion, put up his pistol and put Phelan ashore. Phelan made his way back to New York, when he again shipped for Brazil as quartermaster of a vessel, making the round trip and saving eighty dollars in money. With this he returned to Memphis and again proposed to practice law, confined principally to criminal practice. He rose quickly to prominence in this practice and seemed destined to great success. In 1870 he published, in the Memphis *Appeal,* a column article attacking with great point, vigor and sarcasm the then Democratic executive committee. It was especially caustic on James Brizzolari, a young Italian, a lawyer and member of the committee, and making himself prominent in local politics. Brizzolari published a bitter personal denunciation of Phelan and Phelan challenged him at once. A duel took place between them across the river and just below Memphis. It was witnessed by the passengers of a steamer, many ladies being witnesses. Two shots were fired, when at the second Brizzolari fell, wounded in the shoulder. Phelan was again the lion of the hour. His second in the duel slept with him the night before. He relates that at pipe of day that morning, he was awakened by Phelan springing out of bed crying, in the language of Hotspur: "The sun doth gild our armor; up my lords."

In October, 1872, he married Miss Julia Hunt, the beautiful daughter of Colonel W. R. Hunt, of Memphis. He subsequently served a term in the Tennessee Legislature; and was quite prominent in the state politics of the next few years. His health, however, soon failed him. Consumption, the dread curse of the race, had seized him, and the balance of his life was a brave, but unsuccessful resistance to its ravages. One season, with only a negro cook, he spent on the prairies and among the Ute Indians of Colorado. Thrice, with a negro attendant, he spent the winter in a small sailboat between New Orleans and Jacksonville, Fla. Often, sick and alone, he would lay for days upon some small island of the coast, hovering between life and death. Finally his physician told him he had but little time to live, and no hope, and he gave up the fight, and came home to die. He died in Memphis in September, 1882.

The story of this struggle for life, known only to a few, has more of courage and pathos than would furnish forth a novel. To use his own expression as to the final surrender, when he was told that his days were numbered, "Then I felt it was childish to contend longer with my fate. Better by far to wrap my toga around me and fall with dignity, than to spend my last hours fighting with straws, and battling for a little more breath."

This is but a brief and meagre outline of the principal events of his life, a poor portraiture of one of the brightest intellects that ever adorned the Memphis bar. Had his health permitted his steady pursuit of his high aims, and his life been spared a few years, he would have attained the highest eminence.

# BOOKS.

ADDRESS DELIVERED AT BROWNSVILLE, TENN.

Among the many gifts of the gods to mankind there was one that is second only to the gift of intelligence. It may be said to be the gift of a good friend—a friend who, more than Bacon, has "taken all knowledge for his own"— a friend, the most learned of all others in the world, one whose wisdom surpasses that of Solomon; whose wit is better than that of Sidney Smith, or humor than Dickens or Mark Twain; a friend who will come to your home and be your guest; a guest without trouble or expense; who will be silent when you wish, or speak when you desire to be entertained; and be didactic, polemic; learned or witty, as suits your own varying mood. One, who, when leaving, if you wish him to leave, carries no story of your house, remembers no skeleton in your closet. This unknown, but I trust, well known friend of whom I wish to speak, is a book, or books.

It is often that we know little of some of our best friends. This is specially so with books. They seldom bore you talking about themselves. The daily companions and teachers of our lives, grown common from constant presence. We never ask, and possibly never know their origin, progress, history, or even present state. Each of these, would. and have, furnished materials for essays, lectures, and other books without number. The story of the invention of letters, the art of printing, the progress of book-making, each of these fill volumes.

The invention of printing, the place, the mode, the person, the invention and the inventor, are each the subjects also of much writing. The invention of movable types is claimed for Faust, for Shaffer, for Guttenberg, for Costar; while Haarlem, Mentz, Strasburg, all claim the honor of its birth place. Haarlem erected a statue to Costar, and Mentz to Guttenberg, while some enthusiast discussing these conflicting claims, declares the invention came from Heaven, brought

like fire, by some Prometheus, the gift of God. Probably
the nearest approach to the truth, as suggested by D'Israeli is
that there were separate inventions in different eras, and
possibly, as claimed by Clements (Mark Twain) for Tele-
phony that it was invented simultaneously by different persons—Bell and Drobaugh—at different places; or invented
by one and instantly transmitted by some mysterious mental
telegraphy to the others.

Certain it is that printing was known in China long be-
for the Christian Era. It is a remarkable fact, that the
three greatest agencies in human affairs, the compass, gun-
powder, and printing, have been traced to the Chinese; but
the mystery remains how and when these sublime inventions
stole over the Great Wall.

Its introduction to England was from Haarlem, where
the secret was so closely guarded, it was necessary to smug-
gle away a printer, Corsellis, to Oxford, where the art of
printing was revealed and cultivated. Then came Caxton,
and after him a long line of illustrious printers and binders,
from the celebrated Elzevirs to Murray, and down to the
Appleton and Harper's of this day.

It was not long e'er the power of printing and the dis-
semination of knowledge by this means began to be felt. It
soon threatened priestly domination and kingly prerogative.
At first confined to a few licensed publishers, its power was
not so great. But under Henry VIII books became the
teachers of the rights of men, the advocates of political and
religious freedom, and the organs of the passions of mankind.

Power-loving Woolsey became alarmed, and the war
against books began, continued with varying fortunes in England, as it did and has in every Government of the Globe, until comparatively recently, the freedom of the Press has been
finally established as a very corner-stone of human liberty.

Every part of a book, even the punctuation, has its history. Every slight improvement, even though trivial, has
its motive, and supplies some want. The "i" was not dotted
in writing, until the 11th Century. Caxton introduced the

Roman pointing, as used in Italy, while Pynsen brought the Roman letters. The simple dash and perpendicular line were at first the only marks of punctuation, and then came the comma, and then the colon; but the semi-colon was too great a refinement until Butler's English Grammar in 1633. The semi-colon was unknown to Shakespeare, and its non-use by him has given rise to much difference of interpretation in many passages.

The progress, in the merely mechanical feature of books has its history, none the less interesting and instructive. Beginning with the crudest form of wooden type as used by Guttenberg, coming next to the movable metal type, and afterwards the printing presses. Then the various folios and the bindings from common parchment, to the modern morocco and calf gilt.

Then the invention of paper, which was first made in England about 1588, by a German who was Knighted by the Oueen. One by one these progressive steps were made, as mankind advances in all mechanical arts, until today, the making of books has reached a state of perfection second to no one of the products of human ingenuity and intelligence.

The art of binding has reached a high state of elegance and beauty. Though known to but few, Memphis has an Artist Binder of the highest order of merit, and known to lovers of beautiful binding in most countries. His binding of a small volume commands as high as $600.00. I refer to Mr. Otto Zahn.

The etymology or nomenclature of books has also an interesting history. Take the word "Stationer" for example. This word was first applied to a class of scribes and limmers and dealers in manuscript copies who had fixed localities or stations in the streets, and from this word "station" came "stationers," and after the increase of books, these were naturally included in the stock in trade, and "book-seller" and "stationer" became nearly synonymous terms.

The most unique modern definition of a book is that of Sol Smith Russell, I believe—"Some printing. bound in calf, with the tale inside."

There are many other interesting facts connected with the history of books, upon each of which many volumes might be written. Accounts of Political and Religious Pamphlets, Libraries, Famous Printing Presses, Suppressed Books, Authors, Publishers, and Lost Books, but the scope of this occasion prevents more than mere mention of these.

Of the lost books, the most remarkable instance, perhaps, was the loss of the Pandects of Justinian. These were in substance a codification of all the best of Roman Law made by the ablest of Roman juris-consults, under the supervision of Justinian, and became the law of the most enlightened and prosperous days of Roman history. Of these Pandects it was justly said, that they were the most precious monument of the legal genius of the Romans; and indeed, whether one regards the intrinsic merits of its substance, or the prodigious influence it has exerted and still exerts, the most remarkable law book that the world has ever seen. But when Rome fell, these fell, and were lost to the world; and this splendid system of jurisprudence disappeared as completely as if it had not existed. It was not known that a single copy existed until the middle of the Twelfth Century, when the Pisans who plundered Amalfi, found a single copy, and this copy today furnishes the ground work for the system of jurisprudence known as the Civil Law prevailing in a large portion of the civilized world.

This copy of the Pandects found at Rome is in the Laurentian Library at Florence, and your speaker when in Florence was able to see but two things—this copy of the Pandects, and the Venus de Medicis; one the most splendid monument of the genius of man, the other the most artistic example of the beauty of woman.

Another important subject in connection with books is that of book-marks. Much time and ingenuity, and no little expense, has been incurred in devising unique book-marks and accompanying mottoes. Some have been handed down from generation to generation and become a part of the family Coat-of-Arms. Some of these are beautiful in design with tasteful mottoes, original or quoted, while others are of doubtful taste. The motto of one fine library in Memphis is this: "He that borrows a book and fails to return it is a thief." That of another good friend of mine, a distin guished educator and woman, whose body now sleeps in Elm-wood and whose soul has I trust penetrated all mysteries and walks among the stars, was from the advice of Laertes to Polonius; "Neither a borrower nor a lender be." One time she sent me a volume to read, and I returned it at once with thanks, and regrets that I could not get beyond the book-mark.

Appropriate matter of a book motto is suggestion of kind treatment and early return. You will pardon me if I give my own composed book-mark and motto. The mark is a book with my name and this motto·

"Treat me kindly for I have a soul,
Return me shortly for I have a lover."

Having spoken thus far briefly of the history of books, I wish to make this suggestion. Parents rely too much on schools to educate their children. They are liberal in their expenditures for schools and colleges, and overlook or for-get the potent influence of the mere presence of books in the homes and rooms of their children. Every house, however humble it may be, should be provided with some sort of book-case, companion to the cook-stove. A former Governor of your great State has sung the triology of the axe, the rifle and the fiddle, and eloquently portrayed their influence in conquering a wilderness, subduing the savage, and advancing the civilization of a great people. He calls up the Genii of the past. The potent age of progress for the present and the future is the book-case. Then when the book-case is pro-vided, let the work of filling it begin. Let books be the anniversary present to the children; give them books on slight occasions; then let each child have his or her own very little book-case. Stimulate their fondness for books, and their making companions of them, and you have at once just so many teachers at work helping the teachers of the school. These silent and seemingly dead agencies will be working

like the corals of the sea, that rear the dreamy isles, mould
ing beautiful lives and adorning cultivated homes.

One of the most cultivated women we have ever met was
never a student in a school.  Reared in the country away from
the petty but pitiless distractions of society, she was fortunately surrounded by books, and from peeping at the pictures
she came to read the contents, and then directed by an aged but
educated grand-father, like Romola and her father, she made
friends with the authors and they became her companions,
teaching her the mysteries of science, the lessons of history,
the charm of romance, and the exquisite beauty of poesy and
song.

The most important thing to learn about books is what
to read and how to read them.  One of the great misfortunes
attending the acquisition of human knowledge is, that few
have in their youth a competent guide showing them what and
how to read.  In all the vast wealth of books, their abundance
and cheapness, few have intelligent directions as to their use.
The educators themselves are too often content with directions to their students as to the text-books of the school, leaving the hungry, ravenous minds to devour any mental pabulum
that comes in their way, but to find later in life that greater
mistakes have been made, and precious time lost in the reading of worthless trash, winnowing much chaff for little wheat,
when rich store-houses of pure grain were near.

The worst effect, however, of this kind of reading is the
effect upon the mind itself.  The mind, like the stomach, can
only retain and digest so much food.  That which it does not
assimilate, it throws off.  Mental dyspepsia has more victims
than cholera.

One of the safest rules is to read only books of approved
merit.  The poet Rogers was wont to say, "When a new book
comes out, I read an old one."  The great Lord Dudley wrote
that he preferred reading books of approved merit, than new
books only to find that they were not worth reading.

Cervantes, in Don Quixote, says "There are men who will
turn you out a book with as much dispatch as a dish of frit-
ters."

De Quincy said one of the misfortunes was, one had to read thousands of books to find out one need not have read them. It will be well to adopt with reference to our reading the maxim of Alphose of Castile, as given by the "Antiquary." "Old wood to burn, old wine to drink, old friends to converse with, and old books to read." "Every book, whatever be its character, may be considered as a new experience made by the human understanding." Ruskin says that books of travel, and of the sciences, are the only new books that should be read by the general reader, and those only after approval of those professing literature. Every department of human knowledge and human thought now has its approved literature. Lists of those classified into Hebrew, Oriental, Greek, Roman and English; poetry, prose, philosophy, are easily obtained. It is too long to repeat here. Of books, it is useless to say that the Bible and Shakespeare stand foremost. Among the vast volumes of commendation of the Bible, none are more beautiful than this:

"Who will not say that the uncommon beauty and marvellous English of the Protestant Bible is not one of the great strong-holds against heresy in this Country? It lives on the ear, like a music that can never be forgotten, like the sound of church-bells, which the convert hardly knows how he can forego. Its felicities often seem to be almost things rather than mere words. It is part of the National mind, and the anchor of National seriousness. The memory of the dead passes into it. The potent traditions of child-hood are stereotyped in its verses. The power of all the griefs and trials of a man is hidden beneath its words. It is the representative of his best moments, and all that there has been about him of soft and gentle and pure and penitent and good speaks to him forever out of his English Bible. It is his sacred thing which doubt has never dimmed, and controversy never soiled. In the length and breadth of the land there is not a Protestant with one spark of religiousness about him whose spiritual biography is not in his Saxon Bible."

French, English—Past and Present, Page 36.
Dublin Review, June 1853.

And this of Shakespeare, this, which, I know, when you
have heard you will pardon so long a quotation.

"In thy tragedies, thou has the majestic grace which
in the Attic ages belonged to Sophocles alone. Thou hast
the stately march and music of Aeschylus, without in thy
themes his ceaseless iteration of predestined woe, which
ranks his heroes outside humanity. Yet the sombre hand
of fate hath not more inflexibly driven the gentle Iphigenia to her doom than it hath followed Macbeth to his
foreshadowed crime and end. But in thy canticles, it is
not an overshadowing, mysterious and tragic fate, but a
gracious and living providence, which as thyself hath
phrased it:

'Holds in his hands the shears of destiny,
And has commandment on the pulse of life.'

In comedy, Aristophanes is not thy Master; yet must I
greatly choose thy tragedies as monuments of thy abid-
ing faith; funeral dolors rather than bridal carols inspire
even the harp of David, beloved of the Lord; and the
pencil of the Holy Ghost touchest ever the shadowed
phazes of our early lives. As the love of beauty and
poesy is of perennial life, so thy memory shall survive
the mutations of time, and shall be the Nation's heri
tage, while fancy and imagination dwells in the souls of
men."

*"Shakespeare's Insomnia"*—Heard.

Men of letters have attempted select lists of Authors.
Those selections have been as diverse as the literary taste of
the parties. Even the recent attempt of President Elliott has
waked widest dissent and criticism. There are some authors
however, of almost universal approval, such as Homer, Demos
thenes, Aeschelus, Thucidides, Virgil, Dante, Shakespeare, Mil
ton and George Elliott.

Of books it may be said they should be like your acquain-
tances, have only a speaking acquaintance with some; make
friends with others, and be the lover and sweethearts of a few.

Of many Pierian Springs, you can do as North said of the Ettrick Shepherd in Noctes Ambrosiane: "You cannot drink; you can only get close enough to dip your feet in."

D'Israelli says a predilection for some great author among the vast number which must transiently occupy our attention, seems to be the happiest preservative for our taste. There is an old Latin proverb, *"Cave ab hominum unius libri"*; Be cautious of the man of one book.

Pliny and Seneca say, read much but not many books. Nearly every great writer and most great men and women had and have some favorite author, whose thoughts and language they tried to assimilate, and whose works became their *vade mecum*. Demosthenes is said to have copied Thucidides eight times. Clarendon made Livy and Tacitus his constant study. Grotius loved Lucan so much, he carried a pocket edition, which he was seen to kiss with the rapture of a votary.

And you must learn to love books. For learning is a marble image, that warms not to life at the work of the sculptor, but the worship of the artist.

To love books, you must know something of their authors. Take Scott's "Life of Napoleon." It can only be read intelligently by knowing the circumstances under which it was written. The book and the author of "Uncle Tom's Cabin," the most exaggerated picture of society, and the most mediocre and over-rated book of the Nineteenth Century, owes its notoriety to a heated condition of sectional hate and puritanic zeal.

We can even better understand the rugged style of Carlisle by reading the story of his rugged life, as portrayed by his wife. The story of Dickens' life shows him always to have "owned the white soul from which evil fell away." The sweet salt of humor which digested and preserved not only for himself, but for the world, in his immortal characters, the good out of every unhappy circumstance that came to him.

We appreciate better, the character of Mr. Micawber and Mrs. Nickelby, when we remember that one was the father and the other the mother of Dickens. We feel the keener the deep pathos of little Dorit, when we know that his, Dickens,' father, spent years in the Marshalsea, the debtor's prison.

The lives and loves of the poets, Petrarch and Laura, Tasso and Leonora, Dante and Beatriche, and on down the musical corridors of the ages give the secret intone of their poetry.

The lover of books gets in return the most substantial benefits, and the most delightful moments of human existence. The pleasure of the acquisition of knowledge increases with usurious rapidity. The acquisition of each high plane of human knowledge broadens the view and adds new charms to the mental landscape. Unlike the mountain tops, "most wrapped in clouds and snow," the reading of one book introduces us to the delightful companionship and understanding of another. It is the delight of youth, the pleasant occupation of manhood or womanhood, the philosophic solace of old age. No age or condition of life but is benefited by a love of reading. The invalid who does not read is to be pitied. The invalid who does read is almost to be envied, for its opportunities. Though confined within narrow walks, such invalids watch the stars with Miss Hershell, and walk Parnassian Heights with Goethe and Schiller; talk with Rogers, and listen to the rounded periods of Montaigne and Macauley; to the simple stories of Wallace and Crawford; and repeat the songs of Jean Ingelow. Thus do many invalids acquire a cheerfulness born only from the philosophy of faith, and by a keen appreciation and transmission of all the charms of letters.

What power, what wealth, what happiness in books! If knowledge be the law that rules the world, books are the repository of that knowledge. If "my mind, to me, a kingdom is," what riches may be stored in this kingdom!

If you wish to travel, without dust, heat or weariness, take Stanley and go through the dense forests of the Congo or the Zambesi. Take Kane and Naansen, and you can see ice-bergs and the Aurora Borealis; or Howard, and you can float down the grand canal of beautiful Venice. Read the House Boat on the Styx, and you companion with Noah and Lucretia Borgia.

Listen to Thucidides, and he will tell you the story of Grecian and Spartan glory. Gibben will follow with you the Roman Phalanxes that conquered the world; and Headley the French legions, the screams of whose eagles were heard beneath the pyramids and on the Banks of the Boristhems and the Po. Newton, Humboldt, and Liebnitz will explain the mysteries of the physical cosmos, and Maury the mighty influence of the gulf stream, and the mysterious wanderings of trade winds and majestic flow of ocean currents; while Hershell and Humboldt will not stop here, but pierce with you through an aerial universe of endless expansion, at which the soul aches to think, intoxicated with eternity.

We deem it an honor, and esteem it as a pleasure to know and companion with the great. Through books we know the great of every nation and of every age.

Time, that has swept away the works of the generations from their place of remembrance, has yet guarded the splendid shadows of their recollections for instruction to the successive ages. We can unravel the memory of the world of old. We can behold the cities that are fallen, and hear the hum of the mingled multitude that swarm in all their gates; the glory of their empire, the pride of their imaginable might rises up in its dreamlike pomp from the night of the past, and we by books become spectators of the works and the destinies of men, whom thousands of years have buried in the dust.

Books are the Elisian Fields whence are gathered the spirits of all the great dead of the past, and whence we can commune and walk and talk with them. In books

"The old dead authors throng us roundabout,
And Elzevirs gray ghosts from leathern graves
look out."

It is especially important that women should love books. It is a remarkable fact, noticed by some accurate writers, that all the famous women of the past, were noted as much for their intellectual culture as their charms of person. Cleopatra and Aspasia were more remarkable for their learning than their beauty.

Giving the first impressions, taste and culture to the youthful mind, she should be fitted by her own self-culture for this high duty. The whole range of past history furnished few examples of great men, whose greatness was not traceable directly to the influence of some great woman.

It is only when one has grown familiar with the contents of a book, the life and character of its author, and the circumstances under which it was written, can one walk and converse, as it were, with its spirit, and commune with its soul. One must go even further than this, and grow familiar with the particular binding, to always and readily recognize the book, just as you must readily recognize the friend you greet by the dress he wears. For example, "The Lady of the Lake" dressed in Morocco gilt, had no charms for me, for she told me her sweet and simple story in the long ago, dressed in simple muslin—when the mimosa and honeysuckle of a country home, thrilled to the love notes of the mocking bird. For the same reason, great public libraries furnish me no pleasure. The loneliest of feelings comes to one in the vast solitudes of the British Museum, or Bodlean Library. One sees the names of Plutarch, and Virgil, Bonaparte and Bacon, George Elliott and Balzac, of Pickwick and the Vicar of Wakefield, but they are all strangers dressed in a new dress and sitting in unaccustomed places. They are not the old friends that sit at our elbow, at our own fireside, or looked down upon us from their accustomed places in our own library. If we open one of these volumes, they do not speak to us in the old familiar voice, as it were, and their wisdom or their wit, do not seem to come in or out on the right place of the page.

In connection with this, personal idea of a book, as being the imprisoned soul of its author, preserving and speaking, like the phonograph, the thoughts and voice of the Author, long after he himself is dead; I have wondered if books did not often get lonesome, and want to talk just like men and women; and I have often, somehow, felt, when taking down an old familiar volume, that had told me its story many a time, that it seemed to be gladdened at the opportunity of telling it again, of repeating its great philosophic or historic truths, or of singing its song or repeating its love story, "as old as the song that the sea sings, forever."

I have wondered if books did not get acquainted with each other, living together as they do; if Bacon and Coke, sitting side by side, do not sometime renew the old quarrels If Mrs. Browning, nestling close to the works of Browning, did not sing to him again, her lover, the sweet Portugese sonnets. And I sometimes think with a sadness akin to pain, of when I and those who love me now are gone, who will take care of these old friends, and keep them together, and love them as I have done, and let them talk and sing to them as they have talked and sung to me.

# ADDRESS.

UNITED CONFEDERATE VETERAN REUNION, MOBILE, ALABAMA, 1910.

### ORATION OF JUDGE L. B. McFARLAND.
(*Mobile Register, April 27, 1910.*)

General Gordon in a few well chosen remarks, alluded feelingly to the bravery displayed by the orator on more than one battlefield, presented Judge L. B. McFarland as the orator for this reunion, and he spoke as follows:
Beloved Commander and Comrades:

It has been nearly half a century since the armies of the South were marshalled in all the panoply of war to defend what they regarded as vested and sacred right, and the banner of a new nation, the Confederate States of America, was flung out to be kissed by Southern breezes and warmed by Southern suns.

It has been nearly so long since that banner was furled and since the sound of the last gun was heard among the hills of West Point, Georgia, upon the banks of the Chattahoochie, and their reverberation came back from the plains of Texas, sounding the death knell of the Confederacy.

We, who were participants in this tragedy and who are now gathered in brotherly meeting again, are blessed indeed to have been spared so long, and to have seen the effacing finger of Time erase the cruel wounds of internecine strife, a dismembered country restored to unity, the passions of hate turned to forgiving appreciation, our beloved South rehabilitated to prosperity, and our purposes and conduct better understood.

I am profoundly thankful to have been spared to this hour, and deeply mindful of the honor of being your speaker today. I am glad to be the guest of a city of such loyalty to the cause so dear to us, the home of Madam LeVerte, whose grace and culture were a fireside theme in the South; of Augusta Evans, whose first novels introduced my youth to the enchantments of romance; of Father Ryan, poet laureate of the Lost Cause; and of a Semmes—whose deeds alone made one arm of Confederate service illustrious—a city of such past history, present beauty and future possibilities.

For years succeeding the surrender the causes and conduct of the war were living issues, and the passions and prejudices of the hour voiced intemperance of speech and evoked violence of legislation; while throughout the whole civilized world misrepresentation and misunderstanding of our purposes and conduct clouded the judgment of mankind. But Time, the great weigher of human conduct, and Truth, the great survivor, have spoken in the tribunal of history and Justice has given her verdict. It was but natural that during the passions and prejudice engendered by so great and such prolonged hostilities neither party could do justice to the other.

It is not when the waves are tossed to madness by the winds—that the great level of the sea is taken to measure the heights of valley and mountain or the depths of the deep, but rather when a great calm is laid upon the waters. So it is only in the calm of human thought and unimpassioned judgment that history has written a true verdict about the South. Emmet, unjustly condemned and executed, properly left his name and memory and his vindication—to posterity and history. Posterity vindicated the patriotism of Emmet, and history wrote his epitaph.

It is about this verdict of history upon a few of the issues and results of the past conflict that I wish to briefly speak:

One verdict of history is that the South was unjustly calumniated for its treatment of prisoners; and the execution of Major Wertz a national murder.

The actual facts as to the treatment of our prisoners are now better known, and it has been shown beyond reasonable controversy that the conditions at those prisons were as good as could have been under existing circumstances, and that Libby and Andersonville were as sanitary as the Northern prisons and that the rate of mortality was as great there as here. The North refused an exchange of prisoners or to send medicines to their sick when it was known that the remedies, quinine, for instance, which were specific for Southern diseases, were almost unobtainable. This added to the difficulties in the treatment of our prisoners, and was the cause of much of the suffering.

Another verdict of history is that the South was correct in its contentions as to the abstract right of secession under the constitution.

Stripped of its unfortunate associations with the question of slavery, and freed from the imputation of bringing on a war to protect this property, and considered from its true standpoint, the issue of 1860 was the same as that of 1777, and the same living, vital issue is before the people of the United States now in this year of 1910—that is, the independence and sovereignty of the several states in matters local, with limitations of powers granted to the Federal Government to those specifically granted; or, in other words, local government against centralization. This was the issue between Jefferson and Hamilton and this is the issue today, and the South has today as much interest in the proper interpretation of the Constitution and the preservation of the proper relation of the states to the Federal Government as it ever had, with greater opportunities for appealing to the reason of men, freed, as the question now is, from the moral question of slavery

But while, as we have said, the verdict of history is this as to this abstract right, it is recognized that the secession of the states at the time and in the manner done was the result of a chain of evens dating far in the past, and that neither secession nor war were desired and only accepted by the South as a defensive necessity, and upon fallacious hopes that if war did result—foreign demand for cotton would demand recognition. Aside from the results themselves, which is ever the conclusive argument upon the policy or impolicy of human action, a calmer judgment would have given greater pause.

Says one of our most brilliant writers, Watterson:

"It was the dream of a most attractive fallacy that a great and powerful republic, resting upon the cornerstone of slavery and the products of cotton, could be successfully set up and maintained in the middle of the Nineteenth Century and over the territory embraced by the Southern states of America. It was a figment of the imagination of a statesmanship which derived its inspiration rather from fairy tale than from experience, observation and travel."

And the Hon. Ben H. Hill, in his celebrated address upon the reception of Confederate flags returned by the State of Iowa, says:

"There was nothing in slavery which could justify the North in forming a sectional party to cripple or destroy it, and there was nothing in slavery which could justify the South in leaving the Union to maintain it."

A careful comparison of the resources of the two sections, which need not be repeated here, and the proper estimate of the value of these resources, even against a people brave to desperation, resourceful to the limits of genius, patriotic—to the absolute devotion of property and life and to a cause wholly just, would have shown to calmer judgment this hopelessness of the struggle.

The belief that cotton was king, and the consequent belief in foreign intervention, which influenced many of our leaders to extreme action, was equally fallacious. It was broadly asserted by these leaders that Europe was dependent upon the cotton supply in clothing its people, and keeping the manufactories going and its wage people fed, and that recognition and intervention was sure to follow. This error was early confessed by Mr. Yancey himself, after his unsuccessful diplomatic mission to Europe.

The diplomatic history of the Confederacy demonstrates the hopelessness of foreign acknowledgment of our independence. The overpowering prejudice against slavery was in superable. The conclusive cause of their not interfering was this obnoxiousness of slavery and the mistaken idea that it was a property and not as a property right, was the issue. This vital distinction between slavery as a property and as a fundamental system of economy, and slavery as a property right, protected by the constitution, not to be interfered with by others, must be clearly kept in mind. This distinction was recognized at the inception of the war by the English minister of foreign affairs, Lord Russell, but later lost sight of by him. It was urged that recognition meant an ultimate reopening of the slave trade, utterly ignoring the provision of the Confederate constitution which declared this should never be. Our accredited minister to England and France was informed that the people of Europe regarded help to the Confederacy the championing of slavery, and when finally Mr Kenner went to Europe especially accredited to offer emancipation for recognition, the success of the Federal armies was then so manifest that both Lord Palmerston and Napoleon III said "It is too late."

Another verdict of history is that whatever may have been the disappointments of the South as to the results of the war and that the Confederate states did not succeed in establishing a separate government, its people, and especially the Confederate soldiers, indulged in no vain regrets, but heartily resumed their relations and duties to the general government, recognizing that in the Divine economy compensation ever follows calamity.

In an address which I delivered shortly after the war on the decoration of the Confederate graves at Elmwood cemetery, Memphis, I took occasion to say that the then recent war was not an unmixed calamity; that with nations, as with individuals, seasons of their adversity were the germinating periods of their prosperity; that adversity, according to an Eastern saying, was like the seasons of former and latter rains—cold, comfortless, uncheering and unfriendly to man and beast; but from these seasons have their birth date, the pomegranate and the rose—and I then ventured the suggestion that in fifty years the government of the United States by the whole people would be in a position of solidarity, har-

mony and union, and our country one of might and power,
among the nations of the earth, and the people of the South
in a condition of prosperity and happiness that would not
have been attained in a century had it not been for the war
and its results.

The great law of compensation that rules the universe
was exemplified in our case. "The changes which break up
at intervals the prosperity of men and nations are advertise-
ments of a nature whose law is growth." It is with nations
as with individuals, "When the gods depart the great gods
come."

I rejoice today to know that the prophecies and hopes of
forty years ago have come true.

We feel and know that there was a Divinity that shaped
the destinies of this nation—rough-hewn as it was. We real-
ize that God moved in a mysterious way his wonders to per-
form; and now, with Moslem faith and piety we say, "Allah
is great, God is Good!"

The war was a surgeon's knife that removed the ulcer
of slavery from the body of this union, with results that no
palliative measure would have done.

Had the Hampton Roads Conference, or any other of
the attempted measures for a patched-up peace and a soldered
Union been successful, years of unrest and uncertainty and
bickering would have succeeded, retarding for many years
the union of the sections, and the growth, prosperity and
power of the country.

But do not understand me as conceding that the South
was wrong in its interpretation of the ordinances of the convention preceding the constitution, or the constitution itself,
or the inherent right of revolution.

I repeat—the facts of history, the logical and plain interpretation of the written compacts of union, are now largely conceded by publicists and statesmen to be with this view
of the South. It must be remembered that the constitution
itself was a compromise upon this question of the relation of
the states to the general government. The lessons of seces-

sion and war demonstrated the misfortune of uniting too loosely the several states forming this government or leaving any question of interpretation to doubt and controversy.

The question being open to difference of opinion and controversy, the North was easily convinced that they were justified in the defense and preservation of the union in forcing by arms this necessary construction and saying, with the roar of cannon and all the cruel voices of war, in the language of Jackson, "This Union must and shall be preserved."

This view gives a better understanding of the motives actuating the patriotic masses of the North, and also vindicates the South and justifies the heroic sacrifices of blood and treasure, and the magnificent gallantry of the South in defense of the right.

It was better, also, that the fight was to the finish and peace made between soldiers instead of politicians. It was no dishonor to be conquered by vastly superior numbers and resources. Heroes of lost causes have higher places in the traditions of mankind, in the history of people, and in the poetry and song and affections of mankind, than the heroes of success.

Another verdict of history is—that the conduct of the war by the South was the most splendid exhibition of patriotism and self-sacrifice upon the part of the people, endurance and courage of its citizen soldiery, and genius and skill of its commanders, exhibited in all the annals of time and history of nations.

The unanimity with which the people of the South, war being imminent, devoted their property, their lives and their sacred honor to the defense of their states, is without a parallel.

And it should be remembered that the people of the South were devoted to this union. Their forefathers had fought for it—the results of the Revolution was their richest inheritance. The war of 1812, and all the splendors of its achievements were assets of honor belonging largely to the South. The war with Mexico, which added an empire to its territory, was largely fought by her sons. The leadership of her son Washington, had preserved the Northwest territory. Jefferson accomplished the Louisiana Purchase, and the statesmanship of Southern men secured the mighty Mississippi. The records of Congress disclose that through all the years of the nation's struggles and the nation's growth, the wisdom of Southern statesmanship and the South's contributions to the judicial construction of the constitution—lent much to the greatness and the power and the glory of the Union.

The South was largely surrendering her share in all this territory, this history and these achievements. Who can deny that through all the fierce partisan conflicts in the halls of Congress there ran a constant, sincere expression of devotion to the Union, and in the farewells of Southern members to these halls the pathos of deep pain mingles with their haughty defiance. Of all the statesmen who left the senate halls, no one made a more forceful vindication of our conduct and purposes or stately bow in departing than our chieftain, Mr. Davis.

These birthrights of territory, of greatness and glory, symbolized by the Stars and Stripes taken from the coat of arms of Washington and embodied in the one word "Union," the South gave up reluctantly; and this was the most sacred offering laid by them upon the altar of patriotism—devotion to their states.

Of the bravery and endurance of the citizen soldiery it is unnecessary and impossible for me to speak in full; and if I did, it would be but a twice-told tale. It is held that valor is the chiefest virtue, and most dignifies the haver. But I should lack voice to speak the valor of those of whom, and to whom, I speak today.

History in her annals and in the voice of her handmaids —Romance, Poetry and Song, has spoken and will continue to speak of their valor so long as the imaginings of men find utterance. It is not permitted by time or circumstance to recount deeds or name particular heroes. I mention but one name, Robert E. Lee. That symbolizes and embodies not only the military genius, but the best personal characteristics and private virtues of the men of the South. His was the culmination of the South's growth and civilization. Of him, Lord Wolsley says:

"I have met many of the great men of my time, but Lee alone impressed me with the feeling that I was in the presence of a man who was cast in a grander mould and made of different and finer metal than all other men. His greatness made me humble, and I never felt my own individual insignificance more keenly than I did in his presence."

Another Senator Hill, has epitomized his virtues and greatness thus:

"He was a foe without hate, a friend without treachery, a soldier without cruelty, and a victim without murmuring. He was a public officer without vices, a private citizen without wrong, a neighbor without reproach, a Christian without hypocrisy and a man without guilt. Frederick, without his tyranny; Napoleon, without his selfishness, and Washington —without his reward. He was as obedient to authority as a servant and royal in authority as a king. He was as gentle as a woman in life, pure and modest as a virgin in thought, watchful as a Roman vestal, submissive to law as Socrates, and grand in battle as Achilles."

Our own George W. Gordon has recently added another utterance worthy to be repeated. He said:

"Virginia gave Lee to the Confederacy. The Confederacy gave him to the world—and the world has given him to immortality."

Men are great just as they embody in themselves the higher virtues of their day and generations. Signs and symbols and story live because of their embodiment of great truths, as illustrated by the fables of Aesop and the mythology of the Greeks.

Lee and Jackson and Davis were great because they embodied in themselves the noblest virtues of this civilization and the highest characteristics of Southern manhood; and it was fortunate for the South that such characters as theirs stand as representative figures of the South of that day.

Another verdict of history is that the conduct of the people of the South through all the trying period of reconstruction and upbuilding of their beloved Southland, and of their ready and hearty signifying of their love for the Union and a national pride in these, their United States.

There is no parallel to this material and patriotic restoration. It took hundreds of years to efface feuds between Highland and Lowland. The Ireland of today is almost as hostile to England as one hundred years ago, and the hatred of Alsace-Lorraine to Germany is as deep today as of the treaty of Paris. True, in the last two instances they were of different nationalities and with distinct racial differences. The reverse of this is one of the reasons of our national restoration. We were the same people, and with the same traditions and aspirations for the future.

But the most potent factor and deepest underlying cause of this ready acceptance of the result of the war and ready loyalty to the Union was, as we have suggested, their pride in its history, their belief in its present and future greatness, and an inherent love of the Union itself.

The material rehabilitation and restoration of the South to its present condition of prosperity and riches is another of your works left to posterity. The demonstration of its growth and present condition under your efforts is found in the amazing figures which give its comparative past and present resources.

You will have left a country rich, prosperous and with potentialities stressful to the imagination. Who can picture the future of the South, with a climate unsurpassed in its variety, healthfulness and bloom, a soil rich in its diversity, embracing all the products conducive to the most luxuriant enjoyments of life and highest type of civilization? Of one product alone, Dr. Knapp, of the Department of Agriculture, has recently said: "The South can raise five times what it does at present, and increase the net profit ten per cent. If you should double the crop, you could own the world and go fishing." Cotton may not have been king in 1861, but it is the South's royal queen of all the products of the earth that clothe and enrich mankind.

Cotton, "Whose blossom is the only flower that is born in the shuttle of a sunbeam and dies in a loom, and whose ripened boll warms and does not chill, brings comfort and not care, wealth and the rich warm blood, and not the pinches of poverty."

With the Panama Canal complete and trade from all Central America and the Orient ours, with our lowlands drained and made productive, our iron and coal industries fully developed, finding their way by water to these new marts, the merchant marine of the world will be in our gulf ports, reproducing to us royal Venice and ancient Carthage.

These, my comrades, are some of the verdicts of history as to how you in your day and generation have acted and wrought.

It was glory enough to you living—to have seen the marshalling of armies, the waving of banners, the shock of contending thousands, to have heard the musket's roll and artillery's thunder.

> "The neighing steed and the shrill trump,
>   The spirit-stirring drum, the ear-piercing fife,
>   The royal banner and all pride, quality, pomp
>   And circumstance of most glorious war."

And then to have felt the thrill of the charge and the exaltation of victorious Rebel yell!

And when you shall have passed away, you will have left a legacy of heroic deeds richer than the mines of Ind. And, I tell you, it is no valueless name to the living or inheritance to your children or your children's children, to have it written that you were one of the heroes of 1861-1865; that you marched with Jackson and Longstreet and Gordon, with Albert Sidney and Joseph E. Johnston, with Bragg and Cheatham and with Stephen D. Lee, Kirby Smith and Price, or that you rode, sabre in hand, with Jeb Stuart and Hampton, or with Forrest, Van Dorn and Rucker.

I wish now to address myself for a few minutes to the young men of the South, especially the Sons of Confederate Veterans.

In a few years, the last of the veterans will have passed away, and it will devolve upon you to take their places. You will have inherited the glory of your fathers' deeds and the material wealth of their construction. Corresponding obligations and duties will devolve upon you, and what glorious opportunities and fruitful potentialities are yours? The rich agricultural and mineral resources of the South must be developed, improved and enlarged to the demands of a period of stupendous and gigantic undertakings. The question of education must be met. The science of political economy, as applied to the present economic conditions and our present international interests and relations, must be studied. The ever-continuing war between ignorance and knowledge, labor and capital, poverty and riches, anarchy and order, will create great issues whose proper solving will determine the final question of popular government. The true revelation of the states to the federal government under the constitution is yet to be fixed more definitely. The position which these Southern states in their relation to and comparison with the other states of the Union, the place occupied by the South in every department of human progress, will depend upon the characteristics, the habits, the industry and the genius and the patriotism of these Sons of Veterans.

Your fathers will have left you alone. Already Matthew Maury, highway builder and charterer of the sea and mapmaker of the currents of wind and wave, has himself sailed the uncharted and unknown sea. The voices of Lamar and Hill, George and Garland, are no longer heard in the halls of Congress. Mr. Davis, Judah P. Benjamin and Judge Reagan sit no longer in the councils of our people. Dr. Palmer and Bishop Galloway no longer adorn the pulpit and the rostrum. These, and hundreds of others, illustrious in every field of human endeavor, have passed away. Atlas has gone to the

Hesperides, and who is to uphold the world—Ulysses has gone upon his weary wanderings, and who is left to bend his mighty bow?

The answer is, the Sons of Confederate Veterans. Who can doubt that these sons, springing from such sires, will do? Or—

> That we may go down to death
> Cheered by the thought
> That after us the majesty of man
> Will live, and be maintained by other hands.

The traditions of the past, the legends of all our wars and battles, the story of the South's achievements in science, art, agriculture and statesmanship and mastery in all the arts of war, the very atmosphere of greatness which they breathe —strengthen them to endeavor. Our Valhalla is full of the names and memories of great men; the many battle-fields where their fathers fought are here. The marble monuments to the heroes of every battle which centre the marts of trade and rise in every cemetery, the myriad mounds on hill and mountain top—in peaceful valley and by every river of the South—mounds upon which in recurrent seasons the snow lies softly and the grass springs green upon the heroes' graves—all, all, must inspire to high thoughts, noble endeavor and great deeds. The coming times will demand such men.

> "God give us men! the time demands strong minds,
> Strong hearts, true faith and ready hands;
> Tall men, sun crowned, who live above the fog
> In public duty and in private thinking."

A word about and to our Southern women. I will not attempt to recount their heroic sacrifices or eulogize their virtues, their patriotism, their greatness of character or graciousness of manner. Someone has said that "If man's noisy patriotism but one-half equalled the patient heroism of women, no nation would decay, no state perish," and some graceful poet has said that the maiden who binds her warrior's sash, the wife who girds her husband's sword, and the mother who breathes brave farewells to her son sending them to war.

"Sheds holy blood as e'er the sod
    Received on Freedom's field of honor."

But what I do want to say is that the men of the South
owe it as a duty to themselves, a tribute to virtue, and to the
sisters and wives and mothers of our Confederacy, to rear a
fitting monument to their memory. This monument should
be the masterpiece of man's art and architectural skill and
taste. The Minerva of Phydias was the highest expression of
Grecian art and was the admiration of the world, typifying
as it did the beauty and majesty of Woman, a goddess. The
people of Croton gathered together all their most beautiful
maidens that from their combined charms Zeuxis might fashion a perfect Helen.

So let the people of the South rear a temple to the Southern woman, embodying all the best of beauty, of virtue, of
grace and grandeur in architecture, more beautiful than the
Parthenon of Athens, and crown it with a statue to woman
more perfect than Pallas Athena—this monument to be for all
time a temple where Southern women, like vestal virgins, may
keep alive the altar fires of patriotism and liberty.

Now, a final word, my comrades

You remember how, after each battle was fought and
the roll was called—how many noble forms were missed from
the ranks and how as many names were called to which no
answer came, there was a silent response in thought of how
nobly they had died upon the field of honor. You remember
how, after each successive battle, the number responding at
reveille and muster became fewer and fewer, until finally at
Appomatox and Greensboro, Tupelo and in Texas, the ranks
had thinned to only a few bronzed and scarred veterans. So,
at these reunions at each successive meeting, year by year, the
numbers are fewer and fewer. In the battles of life they are
falling, one by one, as they fell upon the other battle fields.
We are dropping, dropping, hour by hour, like the leaves of
autumn. Our farewells each year are the last to many. It was
a custom among the Roman gladiators in the arena—prepared
for contest to the death, to turn to the emperor and repeat,
"We, who are about to die, salute you!"

We, who are about to die, salute you!
Was the gladiator's cry
In the arena, face to face with death
And with the Roman populace.

So, my comrades, we must remember that when this meeting is over and we come to say our farewells to each other, it must be our "morituri salutamus." Let this, our meeting, therefore, be that of comrades and brothers before a long farewell; but let our parting be not without hope of meeting again, and being marshalled again under the blessed banner of the Prince of Peace.

# THE REUNION ORATOR.

### (*Editorial—Mobile Register, April 26, 1910.*)

Judge L. B. McFarland of Memphis, Tenn., who has been selected by Commander in Chief Evans to deliver the annual oration to the convention of the United Confederate Veterans, is one of the foremost lawyers of Memphis, and enjoys an enviable reputation as a lawyer, while his record as a Confederate soldier is second to none. He is expected to make an address to his old associates which all will enjoy and which will supply food for thought for many days.

In order that there might be no interruption it was decided that the address of Judge McFarland should be delivered on the afternoon of the first day of the reunion— Tuesday.

Judge McFarland is a native of Haywood County, Tenn. He enlisted in the Confederate army at the age of eighteen, in May, 1861, in the Ninth Regiment of Tennessee Infantry, and of which he was appointed sergeant major and served in that capacity until 1863, when he was made a lieutenant of his company. Soon after this his regiment was consolidated with the Sixth Tennessee Infantry. The consolidation causing a surplus of officers, he was relieved from duty with his regiment and was assigned to duty as an aid-de-camp on the staff of General George Manney. He gallantly participated in every battle in which his regiment and Cheatham's division, of which it was a component, were engaged during the war, except the sanguinary conflict of Franklin, Tenn., in November, 1864, at which time he was on detached service.

He was an active and obstinate participant in the last battle of the war at Fort Tyler, West Point, Ga., on April 16, 1865, where after a desperate defense of the fort he, with the surviving members of the garrison was captured. Although this was one of the minor, it was also one of the most heroic battles of the war, lasting nearly an entire day, during which, the fort was successfully defended against overwhelming odds, and refused to surrender until General Tyler, the Confederate commander, and many of his officers and men were killed by the repeated assaults upon the fort by General La Grange, in command of a part of General Wilson's forces, which, with largely preponderating numbers, finally overpowered General Nathan Bedford Forrest. Judge McFarland was surrendered, with the little garrison, to General La Grange, who treated him with marked courtesy and chivalrous consideration

The close of the war found Judge McFarland—like thousands of other Confederate soldiers—full of renown for heroic deeds, but destitute of means or money for support and subsistence. But he met the exigency with the same energy, determination, self-reliance and courage with which for four years he had battled bravely for Southern freedom and independence, and was soon engaged in a prosperous practice of the legal profession in which his success increased as the years passed on until he has acquired an ample and independent fortune.

In addition to his ripe legal acquirements, he possesses literary tastes and attainments of a high and enviable order. He is a member of the Confederate Historical Association Camp of the United Confederate Veterans at Memphis and is an aide de camp with the rank of colonel on the staff of Lieut. Gen. George W. Gordon, commanding the Army of Tennessee Department in the Federation of United Confederate Veterans.

# EARLY HISTORY OF MEMPHIS PARK SYSTEM

### By L. B. McFarland.

The Memphis Historical Society requested me to add to its collection of papers, one on the Early History of Memphis Park System.

I have taken pleasure in complying with this request. However, I must premise by saying that our president, Judge Young, in his admirable and valuable "History of Memphis," in chapter "Parks and Promenades," has in detail and so splendidly given to Memphis History the early beginning of our parks, the subsequent establishment of a park commission, and what that commission has accomplished, that it would be a twice told tale for me to repeat what has already been said so well.

I can now only add for your historic gathering such additional facts as to the rebirth and growth of our park system, and my own participation and labors of love in accomplishing what has been done, together with such suggestions of further improvements to be made to the benefit and in the beautify ing of our city which has been my hope and ambition to be done.

The first several decades of my citizenship in Memphis were strenuous years of oppression, reconstruction, and then pestilence, resulting in near bankruptcy.

We had neither time nor capital to do other than struggle for existence, and all the resources of those who wished to render some service in improving the city, was exhausted in supplying necessary requirements.

However, in the latter part of the year 1880, the city had prospered to a condition that it could think of and indulge in those larger and more expensive civic luxuries and improvements that gave pleasure to themselves and invited a larger population. I had from travel and the study of civic economy become deeply impressed with the fact that all prosperous and great cities owed their growth to the potent agencies of nature's gifts, trees, flowers, landscape architecture and public parks.

They demonstrated that the beautiful was the most potent agent inviting and stimulating civic growth.

It occurred to me that the time was ripe for our citv's availing itself of this powerful agency, and I expressed my views on the subject in an article published by the Appeal on the 29th of December, 1889, as follows:

**MEMPHIS PARKS.**
SOME INTERESTING SUGGESTIONS.

(*Appeal, Dec. 29, 1889.*)

*To the Editor of The Appeal*:

We are to have a new administration of our municipal government shortly. This administration will begin under different circumstances and more favorable auspices than ever did one before. There is an era of prosperity and growth upon us, such as we have never seen. Without reflecting upon past administrations and methods, but admitting for our present purpose that these have been the best that the circumstances then allowed, we must nevertheless now recognize the fact that the present and future of Memphis demands a change in governmental views and policy. Our debts and our poverty with low assessable values have heretofore demanded the most economical administration, and this confined to the simplest needs of a city. But henceforth if we would keep pace with our own growth, a broader and more comprehensive policy must be inaugurated.

Other needs besides mere police and paving must be attended to. It is to one of these needs this paper is directed, that of public parks. It is hardly necessary to insist this is a need of any city, scarcely secondary to any other. This need has been recognized by nearly every city of any importance in the civilized world. It may be said that no city will be greatly populous or truly great without proper provision for the pleasurable and the aesthetic. Pleasure grounds and places of amusement are as much of a necessity to the health and happiness of a people as pavements and sewers. Private and corporate enterprise has quickly responded here to this demand for places of public recreation. The Tennessee and Athletic Clubhouses, the new Opera House and Cossitt Library are private responses to this need.

Our municipal government must catch this spirit of progress and respond to the demands of the occasion by providing us with public parks commensurate with the growth and greatness of our city. Every consideration of health, need and pride demand these; and at any price. They can be provided now cheaper than ever hereafter. Fortunately we have the grounds ready at hand. The greater portion of the bluffs, originally intended for parks and promenades, and which should never have been destined for custom-house or library, or desecrated by a shanty engine-house, and be quickly and cheaply converted into beautiful parks by systematic efforts. Let the unsightly engine-house be removed, and all the squares graded or terraced and laid out in walks, sown in grass and planted in shade trees.

Then, let the grounds occupied by the Memphis & Charleston Railroad depot and shops be bought or condemned for a public park, and the depot and shops removed to South Memphis, where they belong and must ultimately go. These grounds are, of all others in and around Memphis, most suitable for a public park. It is in the heart of the city. It is beautiful for the purpose. It is comparatively unimproved. As now used it is an ugly blot. It is an obstruction to communication between the business and a large portion of the most desirable residence parts of the city. It depresses the value and renders less desirable a large area of the finest portion of our suburbs. Convert this into a park and how beautiful and delightful for residences would be all this entire territory south of Poplar and north of Union. The stately houses of the Neely's and Fontaine & Goyer and Galloway, and even to Montgomery's, and all the fair and tasteful residences in this territory would be more and pleasantly accessible and more desirable every way. It would pay the property owners within the area designated to buy these grounds and make a park of them.

As to the means of doing this, there will be no difficulty in having the next legislature provide for the purchase or condemnation of this ground for this public purpose, and for the issuance of bonds to pay for it, if necessary.

But as to the best way to pay for these parks we express no opinion now. It is for the new administration to devise the means. If it cannot, then it is not equal to the occasion and the demands of their offices.

We conclude these suggestions by summarizing: That Memphis must have parks; that they can be provided as suggested above; that it is within the power of the press of Memphis, voicing the public sentiment, to persuade to the effort and then crown it with success.

L. B. McFarland.

Memphis, Tenn.,
Dec. 27, 1889.

At the date of the publication the city was governed by a taxing district with a president not favorable to such improvements, and no attention was paid to the subject; and ten years afterwards while he was vice-mayor under Williams he, with one other, were the only ones who voted against the ordinance establishing the Park System.

In 1898 so soon as J. J. Williams and Hugh L. Brinkley with other broad minded citizens, including H. H. Litty, came into office, the subject of extension of our city parks was being discussed, including the securing the grounds occupied by the Memphis & Charleston Road in the heart of the city, and these being my hobbies and objects of my ambition, the Appeal on the 3rd of August, 1898, published the following interview with me:

A PARK IN MID-CITY.

Why Not Purchase the Southern Railroad Yards? It Would Enhance Values. Negotiations Along this Line Have Already Been Initiated by a Progressive Citizen of Memphis.

(*Appeal, Aug. 3, 1898.*)

Judge L. B. McFarland is serious in everything he undertakes.

He has long entertained the opinion that the ground now occupied by the Memphis & Charleston Railroad for yards, shops and tracks in the heart of the city should be used for park purposes, and lately he has taken some steps looking to the inauguration of a movement in that direction. Therefore something may be heard to drop soon.

Judge McFarland says the time is ripe now for the deal. He says also that whatever may be the cost of the transaction it will amply pay the city in dollars and cents.

The Judge is a firm believer in parks, and that the worst species of shortsightedness in a city government is that which neglects opportunities for picking up eligible park sites when the occasions offer. He points out that as cities expand the necessities for parks become more pressing, and only then it is discovered that the desirable park property is covered by permanent improvements which cannot be purchased or condemned except at a ruinous price, whereas a judicious administration of the city earlier in its history would have seen to it that this land was bought up at a time when it would cost next to nothing.

"The Memphis & Charleston road," says Judge McFarland, "occupies land in the very center of the city, where it gives a sooty, grimy appearance to the very part of the citv that should in fact be the handsomest. Out beyond the Memphis & Charleston yards and tracks, say from Adams Street south to Vance, lies all the best residence portion of Memphis, but persons passing to and from their homes out there are compelled to pass this unsightly spot and to risk their lives at dangerous railroad crossings.

"If that property were made into a park, think how property would be enhanced. Residents out beyond would have the pleasure of passing through the most delightful part of the city going to and from their homes, and those who traveled in vehicles, instead of facing the terrors of a railroad crossing, would journey through the shade and over a park driveway. And then think of the effect of such a park on strangers. As it is now, when we wish to show strangers the residence streets of the city we have to carry

them through the disagreeable railroad yards.   If we had
the park they would first journey under the shade of great
umbrageous trees and then the elegance of our residences
would burst upon them.   The effect would be magnetic.

"I have no idea what it would cost to buy that land from
the Memphis & Charleston Company, but it would not be too
much whatever the figure.   Think of the enhancement of
values.   Every piece of realty between Adams and Vance
Streets, as far east as the outermost suburb, would feel an
advance of values from 10 to 30 per cent.   The property
owners could afford to pay a reasonable tax for a few years
to meet the expense.   I should say the company owns eight
acres of ground north of Vance Street, and it should not be
held at an exorbitant price, especially in view of the fact that
there is plenty of opportunity now for the company to secure other entrance to the city.   The company controls a right
of way on Broadway and could easily secure yard room in
South Memphis, where it would be in close touch with the
connecting lines of road that center here.

"I am a great believer in the aesthetic as applied to cities.
I consider it as important an element as in a private residence,
and even more so.   The city that is attractive in appearance
has the advantage over the city that is not, and I believe that
our population today would be as much as 20,000 greater
than it is had our authorities in times past carried out the
plans originally contemplated for the beautification of the
river front.   Twenty years ago there was not a building
along there and the purpose was entertained of making a
park from Poplar Street south to Monroe and Union.   About
that time the Confederate Memorial Association was prepar-
ing to erect a monument.   I was Chairman of the Monument Committee appointed to erect the monument, and we
asked the City Council to give to the association that part of
this river front between Union and Monroe, upon which
the engine house now stands, as the situs for the monument.
We had plans fully drawn for an elaborate Forum.   We
were to have a large marble platform, that was to be used
for outdoor public speaking.   On the rear of the monument,
a superb shaft was to rise, and at each corner of the plat-

form a pedestal was to stand, each to support a bust of a Confederate hero. We were to plant trees and flowers, lay out walks and parterres, put a fence up, and otherwise protect and adorn the place; and that was to be the beginning of the series of parks that was to extend the length of the river front. But obstacles prevented the Memorial Association from using that ground, and the monument was put up in Elmwood. Since then nothing in the way of park making has been done, but the Custom House, library and the engine house have been put up, so that the elaborate part is now out of the question entirely.

"Now, suppose that part had been in existence all these years, how many people would have been attracted here bv the restful spectacle presented by that river front park, to those passing by on river and rail?"

It only remains to be said that Judge McFarland has had some conversation with officials of the Southern road, and has written a letter to the president of that company, initiating the negotiations over the purchase of the railroad property for the purpose suggested."

In the Fall of 1898 just before the meeting of the Legislature, Mayor Williams had prepared a bill authorizing the City of Memphis to issue bonds for the purchase and condemnation of lands for parks and parkways and the election of a Board of Park Commissioners.

This act was passed by the Legislature March 27, 1899. On the 8th of February, 1900, Mayor Williams submitted a message to the City Council recommending city acquiring suitable grounds for parks; and on the 5th of July, 1900, an ordinance was passed on 3rd reading in accordance with the Mayor's recommendation of 8th of February, 1900, providing for parks and the appointment of a Park Commission, and on the same date Mayor Williams placed in nomination the names of the following gentlemen as members of the Park Commission as provided for in the ordinance: L. B. McFarland for the six year term; Robert Galloway for the four year term; and John R. Godwin for the two year term (Minute Book E. p. 400).

On September 13th, 1900, the Park Commission met
and the following proceedings were had; Regular organization was perfected. Mr. Galloway nominated Mr. L. B. Mc-
Farland for position as chairman for two years, which was
seconded by Mr. Godwin; Mr. McFarland was declared
elected.

The organization perfected, the Commission had before
them to secure funds to work with; then to select and purchase the land for the park, and elect a landscape architect.
These details are given in the further statements herein.

We had no difficulty in agreeing at once upon Lee
Woods—and, as I was well acquainted with the Lees of
Nashville, I was sent to Nashville to negotiate a purchase
from Mr. Overton Lee, son of John M. Lee whose wife was
a grand-daughter of Judge John Overton. We were successful in purchasing this tract of some 335 acres for $110,000,
or about $330 per acre, and subsequently purchased other
tract of some 427 acres, fronting on the Mississippi River
about 4800 feet. This tract is well portrayed in the "History of Memphis," by Judge Young, as "Broken into deep
winding dells at frequent intervals heavily wooded without
with wide expanse of almost level plateaus  *  *  *  affording natural scenery of wierd and strange beauty,  *  *  *
when the flowers bloom and the mocking birds sing and Nature seems in silent contemplation to adore one of the mightiest handiworks of the Creator, the greatest inland river of
America."

So fascinating was this to our much appreciated histo-
rian, Judge Young, that he, not satisfied with prosy line,
dropped into poetry (like Mr. Wegg), and sang some really
exquisite verses, as rippling as the rills of these wilds, in further portrayal of this charming retreat.

The most important matter for consideration was the
Parkway, a belt line which the Commission early determined
to establish, accessible to every portion of the city, and connecting Overton and Riverside Parks.

This took much time in selecting and acquiring the right
of way.

In order to interest the citizens and induce donations
of the right of way we selected and surveyed two rights of
way, one along the line now occupied, and the other about
half a mile further out, and both far enough out to run
through as large tracts as practicable, that would be increased
in value by location of Parkway and invite donations. This,
with some advertising and arousing competition of lands on
both surveys resulted in donation of most of the right of
way and acquisition at an expenditure of only a few thousand dollars of the entire route of over eleven miles in length
and embracing 182.23 acres.

The Commission adopted the route nearest the city. The
Scimitar of date July 25th, 1902, published an account of this
solution of

### ROUTE FOR DRIVEWAY.
#### (*Scimitar, July 25th, 1902.*)

The commission took a very important step this morning when it adopted the route of the proposed boulevard or
driveway, the latter name being substituted for the former.
The route was proposed by Judge L. B. McFarland, chairman of the commission. In presenting it Judge McFarland
said he deemed it the most feasible connection between Overton Park and Riverside. The route, as recommended by
Judge McFarland and adopted by the commission, is set forth
in full elsewhere in this article. This route may not be the
final one, as the ability of the commission to get rights of
way will cut an important figure in the matter. But no
serious opposition along this line is anticipated, and if none
develops the driveway, as proposed in the McFarland resolution, will be the physical connection between East Park and
Riverside.

Judge McFarland has given the question of a connection
between the two properties considerable thought, and it is
his opinion that the route set forth in his resolution is the
most practicable as well as the best adapted to all the requirements of a driveway in the matter of beautification and development.

### A DRIVE OVER THE ROUTE.

Landscape Artist, George E. Kessler reached the city this morning and was present at the meeting of the commission. Immediately after the meeting Chairman McFarland and Mr. Kessler drove over the entire route of the driveway. Mr. Kessler had never been over the route and Chairman Mc- Farland wanted him to see it."

This route was also selected with a view to invite selection and erection of handsome homes adorning their grounds on both sides of the Parkway by having it run between higher ground where practicable. Results, it will be seen, approve the wisdom of this forethought, and the fortunate employment of an able Landscape Architect.

The Memphis Morning News of May 4th, 1902, published an interview with me which gives some facts as to the progress of construction of Parks which we used.

### PROGRESS OF MEMPHIS PARKS.
#### By L. B. McFarland, of the Park Commission.
##### (*Memphis Morning News, May* 4, 1902.)

The creation of public parks for the City of Memphis has just begun. With communities, as with individuals, the aesthetics, the study of the philosophy of taste, the cultivation of the science of the beautiful in nature and art, is postponed until prime necessities of life are attained. It was Mr. Buckle, I believe, who said that it took three generations of a progressive race to attain the period of a cultivated class. The first generation is engaged in the subjection of the country; the second, the obtention of competency; and the third has the means and the leisure for cultivation of the arts and sciences. It has been so with Memphis. Its first period saw only the initial construction of a city. Its second period, the accumulation of a material wealth that should now permit the cultivation of the beautiful.

The first proprietors and founders of the city were, however, men of broad views and far-seeing sagacity. They realized the necessity and the advantage of public parks, and to them were we indebted for the parks in the city, including Court Square, the fairest jewel upon its breast, and also including the squares between Front and the river. These last were donated for parks, and the shortsighted, utilitarian and uncultivated policy of previous administrations, which has permitted these squares, with their almost limitless possibilities of beauty, to be taken for an unsightly engine-house, and more sightly, but inappropriately located library and custom house, is to be deeply regretted.

We may hope that now, after many years of retardation, first by the four years war and the consequent years of reconstruction, and then by pestilence, we have fully arrived at the third period of the city's history and growth, that of cultivation and adornment, both individual and community, and the highest exponent and visual demonstration of that community cultivation should be in the parks.

The people themselves have been hoping for these for years. Comparison with other cities of less wealth, less cultivation, and poorer possibilities, has impressed the necessity of parks for Memphis, but it was not until within a few years back that this public opinion impressed itself upon municipal administration with force sufficient to demand action.

### CREATION OF PARK COMMISSION.

In 1899 an act was passed at the instance of the present administration, providing for a park commission, for the issuance of bonds, and for the purchase of lands and creation of parks.

This commission was appointed, the bonds have been issued and sold, and with the proceeds two splendid bodies of land have been purchased, one of about 450 acres, on the river, southwest of the city, known as Riverside Park, and the other, 337 acres northeast of the city, known as East Park.

It is exceedingly fortunate for the city, for the present and the future, that these two bodies of land should have remained vacant of improvement for so many years, until the time was ripe and the day opportune for their acquisition for this purpose, when they could be acquired for their actual value as land, with no payment for improvements which would be valueless. They are both splendidly situated and diversely suited to the purpose.

## TWO MAGNIFICENT PARKS.

East Park is in the extreme northeast corner of Greater Memphis. It is mostly covered with a glorious growth of stately trees and virgin forest, with enough of clearing for meadow and play-grounds, while through its center runs a stream which will be utilized, for bodies of water to give completeness and diversity to the landscape. The ground is rolling, and one commanding hill furnishes location for the improvements that are to be erected, and from which beautiful vistas stretch in every direction and stream and wood can be enjoyed.

The other, Riverside Park, is on the river. It begins at the southern boundary of the city and extends a mile and a half along the river bank, and having a width of about half a mile. It is almost wholly cleared and much broken, giving full scope to the highest genius of the landscape architect and promising possibilities of splendid culture. Its treatment will be the antithesis of that of East End. The views from the bluffs, which form its western boundary, across and up and down the river are extended and pleasing. It may safely be predicted that in the future, when this park has been improved, good driveways have been extended to it, and when pleasure boats run from the city wharf to its gates, it will be the most beautiful and charming pleasure ground on all the miles of the Mississippi.

## FORREST AND GASTON PARKS.

In addition to these is Forrest Park, some nine acres near the center of the city, so named for Gen. N. B. Forrest, and in which will be erected the equestrian statue of that great cavalry leader. It is the design of the commission to subordinate everything except its utility as a park in the treatment of these grounds to the fact that it is Forrest Park and to the accentuation of the monument itself.

There is also Gaston Park, some five acres in the southern portion of the city, donated by John Gaston, which will make a beautiful small park. This park has just been graded, set in trees and sown in grass.

It has only been a few months since the commission was furnished with money for the purchase and improvement of parks.

Their first work was the selection of a landscape architect whose capacity and experience fitted him for the work before them, and after much correspondence and investigation as to his fitness they employed George H. Kessler, of Kansas City, Mo., an eminent landscape architect, who has planned the extensive park system for Kansas City and parks in other places, and he has gone actively to work on the Memphis plans.

A corps of engineers has been at work for several months making preliminary topographical surveys of each of the parks preparatory to the architect's studies and plans. This survey has been completed for Gaston and East Park, and the engineers are now at work on Riverside, and so soon as they have finished this they will go to Forrest Park. We have established a nursery at Riverside and have planted out some 50,000 young trees for transplanting in the parks.

Mr. Kessler, the architect, is now engaged on his plans for East and Forrest Parks, and work will follow next on Forrest and East Parks. Later the smaller parks in the city will be taken up and improved as rapidly as possible.

### BOULEVARD SYSTEM PLANNED.

In addition to the work to be done upon these parks, the commission intends to connect them with a system of boulevards, one running from the north line of Riverside Park eastwardly to a point south of East Park, and thence northwardly to East Park, and thence westwardly to Chelsea. The route of these boulevards will be selected and surveyed in the near future.

It may be added that the park commission are assured of the fact that they can accomplish but little unless supported by a strong, favorable public sentiment. The people must encourage and help the commission and the administration in this work if they want a beautiful city.

They also appreciate fully the dignity and the importance of the work before them, and they wish to build for the far future and upon broad and comprehensive lines. Their ideas in this respect have been well expressed recently by one of the commissioners for the improvement of Washington City·

"It is not so much money that is wanted to shape municipal improvements in response to the growing taste of the American people as it is a general, a well-thought-out plan, a plan that reaches out not merely through one throw of the political dice, but beyond men and seasons and policies for a century.

"What is logical is also beautiful. The monuments of Pericles, reared in the zenith of Attic supremacy, are logical. The pilgrims of the twenty-four centuries say they are also beautiful."

### NAMING THE PARKS.

When the commission purchased the Lee woods as it was then known, its geographical situation naturally gave it the name "East Park," and so it was called at first, but soon the commission began to discuss the question of naming that and the one on the river. This last was easily chosen and I proposed the name-of "Overton Park" for the other, I was familiar with the history of Judge John Overton, his honorable life, his distinguished character, and his being the father of Memphis parks, and for these reasons and others as given in the resolution passed by the commission in so naming it, I offered his name to our board and urged its adoption. At this time the question of naming the parks became a public one, and the Memphis Scimitar, very properly in public service, suggested that the citizens themselves should vote upon what name the commission should give this park, and arranged and provided coupons for voting under a committee of bankers, and for several months a most interesting contest was waged, and the commission postponed officially naming until the people had expressed through the Scimitar their choice of names. I, of course, gave to the public my choice and the reasons why we had proposed the name of Overton substantially what was embodied in the resolution adopted by the commission naming the parks.

The final count of votes by the bankers was made showing the name Overton led by an overwhelming majority 49,992 out of a total of 80,000. The remaining votes being distributed among a number of other names. This vote was reported to the commission and the following resolution, which I had prepared and referred to above, was offered by Mr. Galloway.

EXCERPT FROM MINUTES JULY 25TH, 1902. MINUTE BOOK "A," PAGE 23.

"Chairman McFarland suggested the propriety of changing the name of East Park to that of Overton Park, and thereupon Mr. Robert Galloway offered the following resolu tion, which being seconded by Mr. John R. Godwin was unani mously adopted.

Resolved: It is one of the pleasing duties of grateful posterity to perpetuate the name and memory of its illustrious ancestors whose civic services, personal virtues, and private worth are worthy of such perpetuation. One of the methods of doing this is by naming libraries, parks, and public utilities after those who have done some service to the community, and whose name has been closely identified with the history, growth, and prosperity of such community. This commission recognizing this duty, and in enjoyment of this opportunity, have determined to name the Lea Woods, heretofore called East Park, Overton Park, after the family name "OVERTON." The founder of this family, Judge John Overton, settled in Tennessee, in 1789, whilst this region was vet a territory, and not long after he was made territorial revenue collector by President Washington. Later on he became a judge of the Supreme Court of Tennessee, and the duties of this high office he discharged with marked faithfulness and ability.

Being a man of sagacity and foresight, he discovered the fitness of the bluffs on our great river to be the site of a great city, and he purchased five thousand acres of land on which Memphis was built. He gave to Gen. Andrew Jackson, who was his warm personal friend, a large part of this land, and the general sold his share to Winchester and McLemore, and the gentlemen were associated with Judge Overton in laying out and developing Memphis. The wife of Judge Overton was a Tennessee lady, by whom he had a son named for himself who was born in 1821, almost at the very date of the birth of Memphis. This son, known as Col. John Overton, who died in 1898, at an advanced age, inherited a large part of his father's landed interests on the Memphis Bluffs, and all his long life he was connected with the development of this community.

Besides this son, Judge Overton had a daughter who married Robert C. Brinkley, Esq., and another who married Judge John M. Lea, all of whom had largely to do with the history of Memphis. Our fellow citizen, Col. John Overton, Jr., the son of Col. Overton just mentioned and the grandson of Judge Overton, has long lived in the city, and has done much service to the state. In laying out the City of Memphis, Judge Overton provided for a system of parks and promenades upon a scale in advance of the then idea of the necessities for these public ministers to health and pleasure. To him the City of Memphis was indebted for court, auction, and the square on the bluff. This commission, therefore, now names this park Overton Park in honor of this name beginning with the history of Memphis and continuing for three generations of honorable lives intimately identified with its growth.

There being no further business, the commission adjourned, subject to call of the chairman.

(Signed)   L. B. McFarland,
Chairman.

(Signed)   A. G. Booth,
Secretary."

In the matter of names, on the 5th of July, 1906, I offered the following resolution as to changing the name of the small park Market Square to "Hugh Brinkley Square," which was gladly passed, and such is the present name.

"Minute Book A-A" Page 135, July 5th, 1906.

Resolved, that the name of Market Square be changed to Hugh Brinkley Square, in honor of Hon. Hugh L. Brinkley now deceased.

The ancestors of Hon. Hugh L. Brinkley on both his mother and father's side, she being an Overton, were connected with the history of Memphis from its earliest settlement.

Hu L. Brinkley was foremost in connection with the charities of Memphis, he having founded and endowed the Lucy Brinkley Hospital and the Anna Brinkley home. He represented Memphis in the State Senate and was always a public spirited citizen. He was, a number of years a member of the City Council and while such, among the foremost in the advocacy of the purchase of parks, in securing proper legislation, establishing the same, and their best friend to his death and this memorial is deemed a fitting tribute to his memory, and same was unanimously carried."

In another paper submitted herewith I refer to the freedom of the Park Commission from public criticism as this had been during the six years of my service. I should in justice to myself refer to one and the only unkind criticism of my service that ever to my knowledge entered the public press. It sprang from this condition: A controversy had arisen between my associates commissioners upon the subject of the distribution of park funds in improving Overton and Riverside,—one owning large bodies of land adjoining Overton and the other large holdings adjoining Riverside.

This controversy grew so warm between the two that it developed into public notice, and naturally found place in the press.

In one of the articles published in the Commercial Appeal, April, 1906, and which referred to a complaint made by Mr. Godwin to the city authorities on this subject, the article added that Col. Galloway had been criticized for expending so much money on Overton, and that I had likewise been criticized "for the expenditure of so much on Overton and the Parkway because it was alleged he is greatly interested in certain recent subdivisions fronting the Speedway"—

It was true that I had approved of these expenditures because Overton was nearer to a denser population than Riverside, more accessible for the people and capable by reason of its even surface, being cheaper and sooner prepared for use, my name had never been mentioned in criticism on this subject.

I at once addressed a letter to the Commercial Appeal protesting against bringing my name in this controversy and repeating insinuations of unfaithful public service. This letter of mine was at once cheerfully published, in justice to me. It was as follows:

"Memphis, Tenn., April 5, 1906.

Commercial Appeal,
        City.

Sirs:—

In this morning's Commercial Appeal, and in the report of proceedings of the Park Board, I find the following:—

'Maj. McFarland has been likewise criticized for advocating the expenditure of so much money on the speedway and Overton Park, because it is alleged he is also greatly interested in certain recent subdivisions fronting the speedway.'

I am surprised that your paper should give publicity, without inquiring as to its truth, to such reflection upon my public services. The whole statement as to my being interested etc., is false.

The criticism and insinuation that my actions in the Board have been actuated by selfish and personal interest are false and slanderous. I neither own nor am I interested directly or indirectly in any subdivisions, or other property near to or to be benefited by the improvements of either of the Parks or the Parkway, nor common to all. I have, in fact, refused to become so interested in several attractive propositions because of my being a member of the Park Board.

I add, that I am not surprised that many good 'men to whom dishonor's shadow is a substance more terrible than death' should shrink from public office when, though they may give years of their best services to the people, disinterested and without pay, they become the mark of slanderous tongues, and these false criticisms and insinuations are given currency and publicity, without inquiry, by reputable newspapers.

Very truly,

L. B. McFarland."

My six years' appointment of term as Park Commissioner was to end in July, 1906. I was then in active practice in my profession, with work then on my hands that demanded my best services, one of like public benefit to the city as the Park System.

I wrote the following notice to the Mayor and Legislative Council of Memphis and at the expiration of my term of office retired.

Memphis, Tenn., June 13, 1906.

To the Hon. Mayor & Legislative Council,

Memphis, Tenn.

Gentlemen :—

I respectfully call your attention to the fact that my term of office as Park Commissioner expires early in July, and suggest that, in order that the Park Board may be complete, your Board should appoint my successor at the earliest practicable moment.

I add that I have now given six years of my services to the City and its people free. These services, though at times onerous and to the interference with other business, have been congenial to my tastes, and a great pleasure to me. I hold that, since such offices must be filled, every citizen should give a part of his life time—as he pays his taxes—as his contribution to the public good.

I served two years as Chairman of the Board, and during its organization and purchase of the park grounds, and the formative period of the Park and Parkway System, and four years as a member of the Park Board, and feel that I have by these six years of continuous service paid as much of service as any one citizen should be called upon to contribute.

In closing these services, I feel that I can congratulate the people of Memphis over the results of these few years work of the Park Commission. The foundation of a broad and comprehensive system of Parks and Parkways has been laid, which in a few years will result in making this system complete and suited to a city of half a million population, and to make Memphis, if supplemented by proper street improvement and home decoration, the City Beautiful.

Nothing remains but for the people to contribute to the park taxes as liberally and cheerfully as they have done in the past, and the Park Commission, under the direction of their able landscape architect, Mr. Kessler, and efficient superintendent, Mr. Knight, to carry out the plans already perfected.

I wish to express my gratification that both administrations of the city government have left the Park Board entire freedom in its appointment of officers and employees, and its purchases, improvement, and control of the Parks, and to suggest that this, more than all else, will assure the successful management of this department.

I wish also to voice my high appreciation and grateful acknowledgment to the citizens of Memphis for their cordial and hearty recognition of the work of the Park Commission. Never, perhaps, in the history of municipal government has any department, charged with such responsibilities, and expending so much of the public revenues, been so free of criticism and so generously appreciated. For this, I feel, that I am their debtor, and not they mine.

Wishing your administration and that of future Park Boards continued confidence and continued success, I am,

Very truly,

L. B. McFarland.

My resignation from the board of Park Commissioners did not abate my interest as a citizen in the progress of the city, and especially in the development of the Parks, and I was greatly gratified that my associate commissioners that remained continued their services with the same zeal discretion they had shown for six years, and that those following have taken up the work with like interest and results.

In addition to the services of our Park Commission, the citizens of Memphis, proud of the work already done, a few years ago took great interest in this work and formed a Civic League, composed of many of our best and cultivated citizens, whose main purpose was to beautify the city. This league honored me with an invitation to deliver an address at the Goodwyn Institute, which I did, and as it embraces my views as to the value of the element Beauty in the progress and growth of the city and made some suggestions as to what should be done, we add copy of this address. It will be noticed that in that address I rejoice in the fact that the acquirement of the Southern Yards for a park has been actively undertaken by Mayor Malone, heartily supported by the City Council, Mr. Galloway and the other Commissioners,—and that I feel its success assured. It is with regret that we have to recall this assurance of success and substitute the statement that although our legislature passed an act providing for condemnation of these grounds and the issuance of bonds sufficient for purchase, and condemnation proceedings were instituted which would have been successful, the Supreme Court having declared the legislative act constitutional,—at a critical moment in these proceedings, a new city administration came into power, the Park System became in its hand a political asset, and the suit of condemnation was dismissed and the act of the legislature, authorizing condemnation repealed.

This was a great blow to Memphis. These grounds, as is shown, were substantially obtained. They would have been to Memphis what Alsace and Lorraine were to France, but were taken away not by foreign invasion, but by our own city magistrates. We still hope for another change in the views of our city administration, and that this obstruction and unsightly spot may be made "a thing of beauty and a joy"

### REMARKS AT GOODWYN INSTITUTE, FEB., 1909.
#### To "CIVIC LEAGUE."

I am gratified at seeing so many present this evening. I will not say, as did Mark Twain, to one of his audiences, "seemingly intelligent audiences," with emphasis upon "seemingly." I feel that your presence is actuated by more unselfish and higher motives than the usual audience that gathers here. Usually, they come for personal improvement and entertainment; you are here, I know, from pride and love of Memphis, and I hope, to learn how you can best serve the city along the lines this Civic League proposes to work.

Cities may become numerically great by reason of geographical surroundings and advantageous circumstances, but no city can become really great until they become healthful and beautiful. They may be places to do business and make money,—mere marts of trade, but it is only after they have become healthful and beautiful and fitted for homes, do they become really great.

There are two expressions of culture, civic pride, and love of home upon the part of the individual citizen—one of these expressions is in the public buildings, the public streets, and the parks and parkways of the city; the other is in the beautiful homes of its people. The public buildings, the broad streets and the parks and parkways are, however, but evidences of the tastes and cultivation of the individual citizen, expressed through the Governmental Agencies, while homes are the expressions of the individual tastes and cultivation. It is of these two expressions that I am expected to speak briefly—your parks, and then your homes.

And first as to your parks—Memphis was exceedingly fortunate in having as the original proprietor of the lands upon which the city of Memphis is built—such a man as Judge John Overton. Judge Overton was one of the earliest settlers of Nashville and one of the foremost citizens of Tennessee. Judge of the first Supreme Court, and afterwards a Judge of the Supreme Court, then called Court of Errors and Appeals. He prepared the first reports of decisions of this court published and the first Tennessee

Reports. He was a friend of Andrew Jackson and his second in the celebrated duel with Dickinson. He foresaw the prosperity and growth of this country, and the advantages of these bluffs upon the broad Mississippi, for the building of a great city. He became the proprietor of the lands upon which most of the city of Memphis is built, but subsequently, gave his friend, General Jackson, a one-half interest. He and Jackson and Winchester, the latter having become owner of a part of Jackson's one-half interest, determined to make a city on these bluffs, and Judge Overton planned and mapped and had surveyed, the embryo city as it now is. With remarkable wisdom and foresight in planning for a city on these bluffs, he recognized the utility and importance of parks and donated the grounds for these parks, Court, Auction and Market Squares, now Brinkley Square, so named in honor of Hon. H. L. Brinkley, who did so much in originating and securing the present park legislation, and Park Commission, Bickford Park and the park upon the bluff from Union Street to Wolf River. This was the beginning of the Memphis parks. Pity it is that lesser men became the arbiters of the destiny of Memphis and permitted the occupation of your beautiful bluffs for purposes other than parks,—that is, by the Post Office Building, Cossitt Library and an unsightly engine-house.

There is a fact connected with these bluffs which I wish to relate. When the committee, of which I was Chairman, was in charge of the erection of a Confederate monument about 1870, this committee did not wish to erect a monument of the ordinary plan, and put it in Elmwood Cemetery. They had prepared a design for a Forum, or place of speaking, after the Roman model. This was to be of granite or marble, some three feet in height, square or oblong, with steps in front and marble pedestal in the rear for the Confederate monument, and pedestals in the four corners for the monuments of prominent Tennessee and Confederate dead. This was to be placed on the bluff and in the square between Union and Monroe Streets, the same upon which the engine-house was afterwards erected; and this square was to be converted into a park. An ordinance was passed by the city

council, setting aside this square for that purpose and naming
it "Monument Square," and such is now its recorded name,
and to such purpose was it the second time dedicated.   When
our committee went to take charge of this square, it was
found that it was occupied by a military company for drill
purposes, under permission from the city for a period of
some months, not expired, and this Military Company refused
to give it for the intended purposes.   The Confederate
monument was built in Elmwood; the square was not improved into a park, and subsequently was occupied by the
unsightly engine-house.   Had this square been made a
beautiful park, as they intended, it would have served as an
object lesson for the improvement of other squares.   The
Library and Post Office  buildings would have been placed
elsewhere and beautified additional grounds.   This old river
front would have been now as beautiful as Confederate
Square on the bluff, which has been recently improved by
the park commission, and Memphis would have been the
proud possessor of the most beautiful river front along the
grand Mississippi, and the original dreams of Judge John
Overton would have been realized.

As we have said, the giving of these parks by Judge
Overton was the nucleus and beginning of the park system
of Memphis, and a grateful posterity named one of the
largest and handsomest parks, Overton Park.   You are all
familiar with what has been done in recent years in the
establishment of parks.   Suffice it to say, we now have the
most splendid system of parks and parkways of any city of
its size in the United States, and I wish, in the presence of
these gentlemen, themselves, to bear witness to the zeal, taste
and ability of our fortunately chosen Landscape Architect,
Mr. Geo. H. Kessler, and also to thank our Mayor, Mr.
Malone, for his ever ready and hearty support of any measure
benefiting the parks.

There is, however, one more acquisition for a park—
one more spot to be beautified, which will be the crowning
effort in the adorning and beautifying of our city—I refer
to the purchasing or the condemnation of the grounds of the
Southern Railroads and their conversion into a park.   This

had been a dream of mine for years, and twenty years ago, in 1889, I wrote an article which was published in the Appeal, urging this to be done, and giving reason why it should be done. This matter has been recently actively undertaken by Mayor Malone, heartily supported by the City Council, Col. Galloway and the other commissioners are zealously engaged in accomplishing this great work; with such universal approval and such intelligent workers as our Park Board, we feel its success assured. In addition to the purely economical and practicable beneficial results to be accomplished by the conversion of these grounds, the question of beautifying the city and perfecting the park system is one of prime importance and commanding consideration. Beauty, as a factor in the upbuilding of cities, is more and more appreciated. Every city that is being wisely administered, is giving greater and greater attention to the beautifying of its territory. It makes more charming the lives of those who live in the city and invites others to come. It increases the health and happiness of the people themselves. The City of Memphis already has a splendid system of parks and parkways. Overton Park on the East, and Riverside Park on the South and West, with the splendid driveway connecting the two, then Forrest Park near the center, the Confederate Park on the other portion of public grounds on the bluff, form a splendid basis for making. Memphis, the City Beautiful. There are two things that are now necessary to perfect this park system, one is to carry out, as far as possible, the intention of the founders of the city, and improve the bluff, as has already been begun at Confederate Park, removing the unsightly engine-house between Union and Monroe and let that be beautiful, but that property already belongs to the city and its actual development can wait, but let the city, at once, become owner of this old Memphis & Charleston yard and convert that into a park and you will have perfected a system that will make Memphis one of the most beautiful and inviting cities in the United States.

The second voicing and demonstration of the taste and public spirit of the citizens is the building and beautifying of the homes and grounds. It is the individual public spirit and civic pride by which a city is made beautiful, by the erection of tasteful homes and giving them outward adornment with trees, shrubs and flowers and all the other accessories—not necessarily stately palaces or broad grounds, but homes of every size and character.

This effort, however, could be greatly helped by Associations forming for this purpose. There is an aphorism in military tactics that the "route step breaks no bridge." This Civic League intended, as a nucleus, for such an Association, and we suggest that these should be formed in every ward of the city, or a club, uniting their efforts in beautifying each ward and in every way known to landscape architecture, beautifying your homes.

The planting of trees upon the sidewalks is especially important. To have the sidewalks well shaded, tempering the summer's sun and adding beauty to streets and home, is of prime importance. This is the main element of beauty in all of the most beautiful cities of the old and new worlds; in this, Memphis is most deficient. One reason for this is the inconvenience and difficulty and the expense to the private citizen of having trees planted and cared for.

I suggest that the Park Commission should establish a nursery of trees, in charge of a competent man, and furnish and plant the trees at a price which would cover the expenses of this department.

This man in charge of this tree planting should also be florist and Landscape Architect in one, and should assist, by advice and encouragement, the individual citizen and the Ward Associations, in laying off grounds and planting of trees and flowers.

Another suggestion. The city should not require, as it now does, that the sidewalks in residence districts shall cover the whole sidewalk of space. The granolith, or other pavement material, should cover only so much of this space as is necessary, leaving balance for trees and grass. This is the rule and custom in the most modern and beautiful cities of the world. This matter will be formally presented to the City Council by this Civic League.

Trees and grass and flowers are the garments with which nature clothes the world and makes it beautiful. "Wild flowers are the alphabet of Angels, whereby they wrote to hills and field mysterious secrets." The mountains are clothed with verdure and the valleys robe-folded in green. With these the God of Nature has made us a beautiful world. There may be larger worlds, rolling majestically, like ours, in space, but I doubt if there is a more beautiful one.

As was said by Dr. Botler, as related by Isaac Walton, the great Angler, over 250 years ago, about the strawberry— "God could have made a better berry than the strawberry, but he has never done so."—so say we of this world. God could make a better world, but he has never done so—at least we have never seen it. But it has been sadly marred by man, in many places. These bluffs were once clothed with trees, beneath whose grateful shade the dun deer roamed, and the red man wooed the maiden, Hiawatha. But man has desolated the beautiful landscape. He owes a duty of restoration to these hills and valleys.

What potent factor of utility and beauty is a tree? Men may build houses and tear them down again, but only God can build a tree, and it takes him a hundred years to do it. How majestic and graceful are trees! How beautiful when first touched with Spring's velvet leaves—when clothed in Summer's green, or Autumn's russet, and how majestic and graceful when they shake down their green glories and stand bare to battle with Winter's storms!

A city is never greatly beautiful or beautifully great, until the homes are made beautiful. The rose must climb the porch, the vine the bower. The trees furnish grateful shade and the flowers swing incense to the air before the sweeter and more hallowed spirit of home finds a resting place or the city becomes—a City Beautiful.

## LETTERS TO FRIENDS.

Memphis, Tenn., March 29, 1914.

Dear Mrs. Neely:

I feared if I should write immediately on my return from Florida, with memories of all your kindnesses fresh upon me its tone might appear fulsome, and so I delayed. I find however, no effacement or prospect of any.

Your beautiful *home* and gracious hospitality is still fresh with me, and of these I write for Floy and myself; and if the write shall turn out a love letter so much the better—it should be a song.

I use the word Home above advisedly, for every house is not a home. There must be a woman, and the woman must have a heart and a soul, for without these there is no home. It is the loving pulsations of the woman heart and the illumination of the woman soul, that like the lamp and the lit hearth, fills the home with light and life.

When one has crossed the threshold of the cottage in the land of flowers and received the gracious welcome of its mistress, and bided a' wee and taken in the surroundings of taste and culture combining the useful and beautiful in pleasing harmony, and has partaken of its hearty hospitality one feels and knows it is a home.

The spirit of home pervades it as the incense of flowers fills a garden—and one sits down and says, "Alabama"—"Here we rest." We are glad to have rested so often under your roof tree; and we shall hope that the cottage home may grow gray with the lichens and moss of time, and its gracious mistress and worthy master be given, life, health and happiness to enjoy it, and that we shall always be permitted,

To subscribe ourselves,

Your Friends,

L. B. McFarland.

To Mrs. H. M. Neely,
Daytona, Fla.

Nov. 20, 1917.

(Letter to son of deceased friend.)

My Dear Howard·

I was much gratified at the receipt of your letter of some days since and should have written sooner but have only now learned your address from your mother. I was glad that you should know and appreciate the deep interest I feel in you and will remember my solicitation for your safety, and high hopes for your progress. May I add my assurance to you that you have not only inherited from your dear father my interest and even affection, but have, yourself, shown qualities of sturdy manhood that raise high my expectation of your future worth.

When I consider your birth and ancestry, the surroundings of your youth, the teachings and example of so noble a mother and wise father and your opportunities of education and the blessing of a fortune that will give leisure for devotion to study and cultivation I can but hope for you a useful future. From such surroundings wisely advantaged by its young men before the war, the South became famous in great men and dominant in national statesmanship.

I am a firm believer in the great law of Compensation, and from this war, destructive and terrible as it is, I look for many compensating results. Aside from its national and political betterments so well futured by our greatest of Presidents and statesmen, the individual and personal strengthening of our youth will be a wonderful factor in our future private worth and national greatness.

I am a great believer in the beneficial effects of early army discipline, made so by four years of army service and personal experience, and years since of observation of the manhood of the South after such training. It teaches obedience to law, not only military, but, incidentally, all law civil and divine. It teaches self reliance and encourages manhood and that "Valor is the cheapest virtue and most dignifies the haver." Had I a son he should have gone to a military school and then if a war, to the front.

I need not add I am glad you went. My only solicitude will be for your health and safety. This last, however, is a necessary risk. My principal fear in your particular case will be of your youthful ardor and overleaping ambition. May I suggest as to the ambition that nothing is truer than the answer of Falstaff to the query—Who hath honor? "He that died o' Wednesday." (Woden, the God of War's day) and the best soldier and truest patriot is the one that risks his own life as little as duty requires. Every soldier who perishes in vain seeking of praise and unnecessarily, is guilty of wasting just the value of his life to his command, his country and his friends and those most near and dear to him. He is a faithless trustee of the divine gift of life.

Pericles in one of his letters to Alcibiades who had been reckless of life says: "Discretion is the sure sign of that presence of mind without which valor strikes untimely and impotently. Judgment alone makes courage available and constitutes power with genius."

There is an old motto from the shield of the bravest of Crusaders, as I remember, that should be the guide of any soldier—"Be bold. Be bold. Be very bold. Be *not too bold*."

You see, Howard, I have usurped parental privilege in being somewhat didactic. I trust you will charge it to the deep interest I have in you.

Very truly,

L. B. McFarland.

To Mr. Howard Stovall.

Note: This young man scarcely of age, volunteered directly war was declared, selected the airplane branch, was sent to France early, made one of the Thirteen (13) Aero Squadrons, served to the end of the war, destroyed Six (6) of the enemies' Aero-Planes in desperate conflict and came home brow bound with the "Ace" honors. He received from the United States the "Distinguished Service Cross" for attacking single handed seven (7) enemy planes, one of which he destroyed and also received the "War Medal" of the "Aero-Club of America."

Battery Park Hotel, Asheville, N. C.
August 10, 1909.

My Dear Judge:

I write you primarily to say that many, many pleasant women have asked me this summer to remember them to you—so many that I have forgotten their names and I now write you for fear that I may forget to tell you they did so. I write secondarily to tell you that you have been a nuisance to me this whole summer—I have met scarcely a single agreeable woman who has not begun immediately to talk about Judge B. and would not think of any other Memphian. "Oh! you know him do you—isn't he a charming man, etc. etc." This began on the train to Tate. At Tate it was repeated by many thousand handsome *widows*—one in particular, from Nashville. The most of them were widows. Then again at Battery Park. I moved on, hoping to get out of your territory—like the man who was tiring of American Ads., sought a place where they would not be found—the loneliest islands of the sea, the wilds of Africa, and finally climbed the highest peak of Himalaya to sink exhausted before—"Take Simmon's Liver Regulator"—painted large upon this most inaccessible height.

I went to Toxaway. I met there a most delightful widow, who interested me much. She was a typical Southern woman of the old regime, in manner, but retaining the glow of later years. I had never seen her before and yet she was an old acquaintance—Mrs. Le Hentz—Augusta Evans and Clemens of former days, and Edwards and Page of later ones described her and told her history under the names of their heroines. Her smiles were like sunshine, or as Festus would say: "Like madiera, bright and warm, is thy smile's charm." And her eyes—you remember them, I know; a man does not often forget such eyes. I could not paint them—no more could the painter limn fair Portia's.

"For having done one, methinks 'twould steal both
    his and leave the work unfinished."

They were dangerous eyes—like Annie's, you remember the courtship of Annie, by Gloster. Having just murdered her husband and children, when she upbraided him with them, he replied: "It was thy lovely eyes that made me do it."

Well, it was the old story—and you bobbed up again. It came about this way: Toxaway was so beautiful, like Mr. Weg, I dropped into poetry—mine was not exactly poetry, but it was rhyme—about Toxaway, and I showed it to this past and present typical Southern feminine. She read it and her comment was: Oh! this reminds me of Judge B. once when we were at Oconomowoc—he wrote a poem about my little boy—it ran thus:

> "See the tiny little tot
>    What dimples he has got!
> What a handsome phiz
>    Is this picture of his."

I will not say this is the exact language but it was of the same tenor and effect and—*excellence*. It was bad enough for you to again make your entry upon the scene to my displacing; it was worse to have my poem forgotten in your doggerel. It was no more to be compared to mine than the humble grub that gropes upon the ground, to the radiant butterfly that reflects the splendors of all the flowers. I fled from Toxaway, after first apostrophising,

> "Oh! tell me, most beautiful lake,
>    With soft waves laving thy shore;
> Can I not some other refuge take
>    Where the name of B. is heard no more?"

by the widows.

Next year I start for the North Pole.

Very truly,

L. B. McFarland.

Judge W. D. Beard,
    Memphis.
Judge Supreme Court Tennessee.

# TOXAWAY.

Penned while spending summer there.

### I.

We climbed the mountains steep,
 Where dun deer scarce could go;
We crept up heights where shadows sleep,
 With labored pace and slow
'Till lo! a palace barred the way,
 Nestling on the marge of—"Toxaway."

### II.

Here on the mountain's height,
 Where clouds are born and lightnings leap,
Where midnight storms and morning bright,
 Their dual birthright keep,
A lake was formed, where shadows play,
 On laughing waters—"Toxaway."

### III.

Here mirrored in its waters clear,
 The mountains loom in aspect brave;
Here, sparkling in each ripple near,
 The sunlight dances on the wave;
And here, in serried rank severe and gray
 Frown the high rocks of—"Toxaway."

### IV.

Here, Nature, in her happiest mood,
 Formed rock and rill and mountain bare,
Here, Art, in choicest humor, stood
 And formed a lake, where coverts were;
A palace rose to bless the day
 With graceful beauty—"Toxaway."

# THE BATTLE OF RESACA.

### (From Battles and Sketches Army of Tennessee by Captain R. L. Ridley, Stewart's Staff.)

A short introduction to Capt. Ridley's account of this battle will explain better the portion of his chapter hereinafter quoted which has references to the brigade to which I belonged.

During the Dalton-Atlanta campaign, on the 15th of May, 1865, Gen. Joseph E. Johnson's army was at Resaca, Ga., with Sherman's greatly superior force pressing upon it.

Gen. Stewart's Division was on the extreme right of Johnson, and was being fiercely attacked, Gen. Geo. Maney's brigade was sent to reinforce Stewart, and was placed on the right of Stewart and extreme right of the army, the 6th and 9th Tennessee, Col. Porter commanding on left, and the First Tennessee, Col. Field, on the extreme right. I was one of Gen. Maney's staff, and he, Col. John F. House, another of his staff, and I were on extreme right with Fields, when Gen. Maney said, "We will go to our left and see if Porter is properly connected with Stewart."

We galloped up the line and when half way Gen. Maney's horse was shot and fell, and Col. House's horse fell, throwing both their riders.

I at once dismounted and offered my horse to Gen. Maney but he said, "No, I will get an orderly's—you hurry to our left and see if Porter is connected with Stewart," which I did and finding Col. Porter properly connected and his regiment (and my old command) in action.

While I was there watching the fight one of Gen. Stewart's staff, Capt. Ridley, came hurrying to me and directed me to pass the order to our brigade to rapidly retire.

In obedience to Gen. Stewart's order given me, knowing it would take me some time to find Gen. Maney, I started immediately down and gave the order as given me, to each of the officers commanding the four regiments, beginning with Col. Porter and ending with Col. Field's; and the brigade retired as directed, in good order—Col. Field wisely forming his regiment in hollow square as the Federal Cavalry was known to be on our right.

Captain Ridley's chapter in his "Battles and Sketches" treating of "the famous order countermanding the former order of attack at Resaca," and directing the withdrawal of his command from the position they then occupied, says;

"General Stewart sent Lieutenant Scott, volunteer aide, to Clayton, and Lieutenant Cahal to Stoval then he called on the writer to go to General Maney. I felt as if that parallel ride from left to right of over half a mile, taking the fire of Clayton's and Stovall's brigades, would be my last. Hooker and Schofield and McPherson, massed, were pouring the shot and shell nigh on to a tempest. I spurred my horse to a run; the balls were so terrific that I checked up a little fearing that my horse might get shot and turn a somersault in falling. The checking process didn't suit for it seemed like death to tarry. I spurred up again and (how any human lived through it I can't imagine) came up with some litter bearers who hugged the trees closely and would not talk. Moments seemed hours. I rode through brush and copse into an open field and finally struck the left of Maney's brigade lying down behind the railroad, hotly engaged. Just in rear of them I spied a staff officer of General Maney, Lieutenant L. B. McFarland, now of Memphis, Tenn., riding as coolly and unconcernedly as if no battle were raging. I accosted him with the query, "Where's General Maney?" He said, "On the right of the brigade," and that Maney had placed him to look after the left. I told him that the brigades on his left were falling back, that if a charge should be made his brigade would be lost, and to pass the order from General Stewart down the line to retire rapidly. In the meantime I started to the right through an open field to find the brigade commander. Talk about thunder and lightning, accompanied by a storm of rain and hail! My experience with bullets through that field was like to it, for "h—l seemed to answer h—l in the cannon's roar." Intermingled with musketry, it created an unintermittent roar of the most deafening and appalling thunder.

General Maney was working to keep the cavalry connected with his line. His horse having been shot he was dismounted but he had taken that of Lieutenant James Keeble, his aide. By this time the brigade was retiring as ordered.

When this order to retire was communicated to Colonel Field, commanding the First Tennessee infantry on the extreme right, the Federal cavalry were pressing, yet his regiment was formed into a hollow square under the galling fire and thus retired with a palisade of bristling bayonets confronting. It was like to Napoleon's battle of the pyramids in squares on the march to Cairo, deterring the intrepid Marmeduke cavalry, and also like the English squares at Waterloo.

But the problem of getting back confronted me. General Maney urged me to stay with him—that it was death to try the open field again. With a detour, however, I hurried back through the storm, neither I nor my light bay getting a scratch. In this short time three horses had been shot under General Stewart and nearly all the staff were dismounted. Terry Cahal had come back horseless; Lieutenant Scott's horse had been shot and had fallen on him, almost paralyzing him; Captain Stanford of Stanford's battery, killed, yet Private John S. McMath was fighting his guns like a madman, and Oliver's and Fenner's batteries dealing the death shots rapidly. A Virginia regiment, the Fifty-fourth, of Stevenson's division, the only one that failed to get the countermand orders, lost a hundred men in a few minutes. The dead and dying of our first line was heartrending.

To confirm the accuracy of my memory I submitted the manuscript of this article to Generals Stewart and Maney and to Lieutenant McFarland. The former refers to it as a very creditable production. McFarland mentions it as a graphic portraiture and makes the additional statement that when he conveyed General Stewart's orders to Colonel Field on the extreme right, he formed his regiment into a hollow square under fire to resist the Federal cavalry, and thus ordered the command to retire. "This was the more noticeable to me because it was the only instance in four years of war that I ever saw this maneuver executed during an engagement." General George Maney replied:

"My Dear Captain: Upon return home, I found your very kind letter advising of your article on Resaca and its having been submitted to General Stewart who approved with compliments upon its merits. With the compliment feature I am most fully in accord. You are, however, in immaterial error in stating that I took Lieutenant Keeble's horse after mine was shot. Keeble's services at the moment were far too important for this and so continued until my command had been withdrawn. It was an orderly's horse I used after my own was shot.

Of course I am greatly gratified at your article's favorable mention of the ever-reliable McFarland and the intrepid Field with his distinguished regiment, and this being only one of many like affairs of the memorable campaign from Dalton to Atlanta which do not appear in official reports, it may be but proper I should say you only saw them as they were upon all such occasions. It was their way.

As to yourself, with memory revived of the stormy hour by your very vivid narrative, it remains but little less than a wonder that you are living to write of the event."

# THE LAST BATTLE EAST OF THE MISSISSIPPI.

*(From Confederate Veteran, August, 1915.)*

Memphis, Tenn., April 7, 1915.

Mrs. W. B. Higgenbothem,
  Pres., Fort Tyler Chapter, U. D. C.
    West Point, Georgia.

My Dear Madam:

Several years ago, you requested that I prepare a paper for you, covering my participation in the defense of Fort Tyler, at West Point, Georgia, on the 16th day of April, 1865, and I promised then, and several times afterwards, to do so, but hesitated and delayed doing so, because of a disinclination to write about an engagement in which I participated, and must, of necessity, speak somewhat of the part I myself took.

Now, after this long delay, I am complying with your request, and inasmuch as I cannot, on account of ill health, accept the cordial invitation of the City of West Point to be present at the Fiftieth Anniversary of the Battle of West Point, on the 16th day of April, 1915, I will give you now my recollection of this fight.

When my command (Cheatham's) was ordered to North Carolina, I was detailed on special duty in Alabama and so soon as this detailed duty was done I started to rejoin Brigadier General Maney of Cheatham's Division upon whose staff I had been serving. I arrived in West Point early on the morning of April 16, 1865. Wilson's Cavalry was then approaching this point from Montgomery. I knew General R. C. Tyler, a gallant officer of our Division, Commandant at West Point, and then on crutches from wounds previously received, and I called to see him to learn if he intended defending West Point, and if so, to offer my services to him. I knew there were a number of hospitals, many convalescents and large hospital stores then crossing Chattahoochie River at this point, and the delay of the enemy was important.  Besides, I had the year previous to this, been in the hospital with pneumonia at LaGrange, Georgia, just east of West Point, and during my convalescence had experienced the generous hospitality of its people, and made many friends, and I could not miss this opportunity for aiding in the defense of these kind people and hospitable homes.

General Tyler told me he intended making a fight, and said his Adjutant was then absent on leave, and asked me to take his place during the engagement.  The General was then starting to the Fort and I went with him.  This was Fort Tyler, situated on an eminence on the west side of the Chattahoochie River, near the town of West Point.  I found this fort to be of simple construction, square dirt embankments, with ditch on the outside, entrance on the west open, and protected only by an embrasure in the rear of the entrance. There were three old pieces of artillery, one a thirty-two pounder on the southeast corner, and two brass twelve pounders, one on the northwest and the other on the southwest corner.  There were no head logs or other parapet protections. We had no muster or muster roll of men in the fort, and I had no opportunity of knowing how many defenders there were, and I knew none of those I found there except General Tyler, Charlie Locke, one of my company (9th Tennessee Infantry) who went in with me, and W. J. Slater, also a Tennessean.  I was informed, however, that there were some fourteen of the Point Coupe Battery of Louisiana, some of Waite's South Carolina Battery, who would man the three guns, and a number of others, citizens and convalescents, hastily gathered.  Then, after the fight had opened, Colonel J. H. Fannin came, bringing in some eighteen more men.  It was a promiscuous, and mostly voluntary, gathering of old Veterans en route to their command, invalids from hospitals, citizens, young and old from LaGrange and West Point, who shouldered their arms and came to the defense of the Fort.

The highest estimate of those who were defending that I have heard was one hundred and twenty-one, although General LeGrange reports two hundred and sixty-five captured, some of them doubtless captured outside the Fort and in and near the town and from the hospitals then crossing the river.

I noticed at once there were two or three nice cottages on the western front of the Fort and not more than one hundred yards from the Fort. I suggested to General Tyler that these would afford protection to the approaching enemy, and suggested to him, that these and all other buildings near should be burned at once, but he stated that he knew the owners, and what to do this would mean to them, and refused to permit them being burned. He himself was later killed by sharp shooters on the top of one of these cottages, and thus gave his own life rather than destroy the homes of others. This was a notable prompting, but was not war.

As the enemy was then approaching, General Tyler directed me to take some twenty men and go out and "bring the enemy in," a military phrase which does not imply physical capture and bringing in of the enemy, but to feel of them and retard their approach. I called for volunteers, and ready response was made by more than twenty, but with the twenty we went out some distance, and I posted the men far apart on both sides of the main road leading to Montgomery, the direction from which the enemy was coming, and awaiting their approach somewhat as Mrs. Partington did, when she met with her broom the high tide from the Atlantic Ocean, and attempted to keep the ocean out of her front door.

This, as I remember, was about ten o'clock. General LaGrange, who was in command of the approaching Brigade, says he arrived at ten a. m. within range of the Fort.

Soon the enemy's sharp shooters appeared in our front, and from thence the "Assyrians came down like a wolf on the fold," and we opened fire along our whole line, and the fight was on, between my twenty and the Brigade. In the meantime, the enemy had established a battery on a hill, some half a mile from the Fort, and began shelling the Fort, their shells passing over our heads. As the opposing force would advance, or "scrouge," as General Cheatham would express it, and the fire would get too hot, we, the picket twenty, would fall back. I remember one instance and shot especially: I had to be along the line directing the stands and retreat, and while passing through an orchard behind our line, and in view, a sharp shooter took a pop at me, missing my head a few inches, spatting an apple tree in line. In mere bravado, I pointed to where the shot hit, and turned, pulled off my hat and bowed to the shooter. Whether amused at my mock heroic pantomime, or disgusted at his poor marksmanship, I heard no further shot near me until I got out of the orchard and from this fellow's range.

We finally got back to the Fort, and as we were in the open for the last one hundred yards, and up hill, and the enemy in close pursuit, our retreat was greatly hastened, so much so was mine, as I always dreaded a shot in the back, especially when running up a hill, that being then on the north side of the Fort and the entrance being on the West, I dropped in the ditch and climbed the parapet of the Fort, and was hauled in by Colonel Fannin, as I afterwards learned it was who gives this account of this incident in the Atlanta Journal of September 26, 1896: He says: "About this time the pickets were driven in under an extremely heavy fire, and for the first time I met .        . Lieutenant L. B. McFarland, of Memphis, Tennessee, in charge of the sharp shooters, as he climbed with his men up the steep southeastern (it was the northern as I remember) side of the Fort, with his fingers in the earthen side to aid him in coming up the steep slope. From Lieutenant McFarland I gained valuable information as to the location of the opposing forces, etc." * * * I have substituted dots for Colonel Fannin's high terms of commendation for me, but take this, my first opportunity, to acknowledge his kind and courteous tribute to me throughout this article of his, in terms dear to every soldier.

When we returned to the Fort, General Tyler placed me in charge of the Western front where I remained during the balance of the engagement. In the meantime, the enemy had surrounded the Fort on all sides, their sharp shooters first taking advantageous positions beyond and on the roofs of houses and in trees, and for sometime it was a battle of marksmanship between our sharp shooters and theirs, the target of each being the heads only of the others. General La-

Grange approached with his right wing through the town, and our gun on the southwest of the Fort took a shot at him and his staff, killing his horse. Finally, his troops being dismounted, they approached and charged up the hill, and it was the attempt to repel this charge that the principal losses on both sides occurred. They, however, finally succeeded in reaching the moat or ditch on every side, and both were in such close quarters that neither could expose themselves to the other. However, their sharp shooters made it too hot and dangerous for our men to put their heads up, as it was almost certain death. A number of our boys would lift their hats on a ramrod and thus get an honorable wound "in the hat."

The most they could do was to keep their powder drv and await a charge. This position of the enemy in the ditch, and our men in the Fort, with only a few feet of earth be tween them, and the enemy's sharp shooters posted in corre sponding position and sniping everything that appeared, continued for certainly more than two hours, and, as I remem ber, from about twelve to six o'clock in the afternoon, the hour of surrender. During this time, our men were not idle. I noticed them repeatedly taking hand grenades, or bombs, the latter I think, cutting the fuse and light them with matches or burning paper, hold the bomb in the hand until about the time it would burst, and then throw it over into the ditch, necessarily quite a dangerous thing, as the bomb had to be held until in the very act of exploding, though, from defective bombs, I do not think many of them did explode.

Nor was either side silent all this time, for Yankee and Johhnie had to pass many a compliment, banter and threat.

Sometime in the early afternoon, noticing that sharp shooters were sniping our men from the cottage on my front, I went back and reported the fact to General Tyler, and suggested he direct a shot or two from our cannon on that side against this cottage, and he walked back with me, and in order to get a better view, stepped out in front of the embrasure and was immediately killed by a shot from one of these cottages. The command then devolved upon Colonel J. H. Fannin, above mentioned, and the defense was conducted

until near six o'clock, when Colonel Fannin called the surviving officers together and suggested the propriety and necessity of surrender, to which nearly all agreed, and a white
handkerchief was run up, and surrender accomplished. We
found after the surrender that the enemy had completely
bridged the ditch with panels of palings and other bridging.

As to the number killed and wounded on each side, Colonel LaGrange, Commandant of the Brigade attacking, in his
official report of the engagement, published in Vol. 103 of
the United States Compilation, entitled "War of Rebellion,
Official Reports, etc.," says: "That our loss was eighteen
killed and twenty-eight seriously wounded, mostly shot
through the head, and that he captured two hundred and
eighteen as prisoners, and his loss was seven killed and twen-
ty-nine wounded." The reports of his several commanding
officers makes an aggregate of their loss as seven killed and
thirty-two wounded, total thirty-nine.

I know of no authentic statement differing from this.
In the official reports above referred to, made by General
LaGrange and the several officers commanding the several
regiments of his Brigade, their statement as to their capture
of the Fort was misleading, in that they convey the impres-
sion that the Fort was captured by their first charge and in
a very short time.

General LaGrange himself says: "The ditch being
found impassable, bridges were prepared and sharp shooters
posted, and when the charge was sounded, the three detachments, vieing with each other, rushed forward under a scath-
ing fire, threw over bridges from the ditch and entered the
Fort .

Again: "The garrison at the time of the attack was
composed of two hundred and sixty-five desperate men, commanded by Brigadier General Tyler," and he then gives the
loss as above.

J. B. Williams, commanding the Batallion, Second Indiana Cavalry, says: "Arriving near West Point we threw out
skirmishers and waited for the balance of the Brigade. At
three o'clock the Second Indiana Cavalry, with one Batallion

of the First Wisconsin and one Company of the Seventh Kentucky, charged the Fort at West Point. The Indiana was among the first in the Fort and captured the Rebel colors."

A. S. Bloom, commanded the Seventh Kentucky Cavalry, says: "After a fight raging furiously for over two hours, I was directed to prepare to charge the Fort. I ordered the men to prepare themselves with boards of sufficient width to enable them to cross the outer ditch. This being done, and everything ready, the Brigade Bugler sounded the charge, which was promptly repeated by my Bugler. My men obeyed the charge nobly, and went charging with a determination to go over the Fort. The men crossed the deep ditch around the Fort on boards, climbed the parapets and went over into the Fort, capturing two stands of United States colors which had been previously captured by the enemy, and assisted in capturing its garrison." *Ib.* p. 435.

Colonel Henry Harndon, commanding the First Wisconsin Cavalry, after stating that one hundred men of his Regiment had been detailed, says, as to the important capture: "The balance of the Regiment, only a portion of the First and Third Batallions, was immediately dismounted and sent forward to storm Fort Tyler in conjunction with the Second Indiana and Seventh Kentucky. The First Wisconsin was the first to reach the works where they lay for several minutes within ten feet of the enemy. Finally the other Regiment got a footing on the works, then the Fort surrendered." *Ib.* p. 436.

H. P. Lampson, commanding the Fourth Indiana Cavalry, says his Regiment charged into the town, capturing the approaching advances. "The position thus obtained prevented reinforcements being sent from the east side of the Chattahoochie River to the garrison of the Fort, which fact a short but sharp contest, surrendered to the remainder of the Brigade." *Ib.* p. 432.

General Wilson, commanding the expedition of which General LaGrange's Brigade was a part, in his report (all these being in the same volume) says: "LaGrange's advances reached the vicinity of West Point a ten a. m. April

16th with Beck's Eighteenth Indiana Battery and Second and Fourth Indiana Cavalry. The enemy were kept occupied until the arrival of the balance of the Brigade, having thoroughly reconnoitered, the main detachment of the First Wisconsin, Second Indiana and Seventh Kentucky dismounted, and prepared to assault Fort Tyler, covering the bridge.

"General LeGrange described it as a remarkably strong bastion, an earthwork thirty-five yards square, surrounded by a ditch twelve feet wide and ten feet deep, situated on a commanding eminence, protected by an imperfect abattis, commanding two thirty pounders and two field guns. At one thirty the charge was sounded, and the brave detachments on the three sides of the work rushed forward to the assault, drove the Rebel skirmishers into the Fort and followed under a withering fire of musketry and grape, to the edge of the ditch. This was found impassable, but, without falling back, Colonel LaGrange posted sharp shooters to keep down the enemy, and organized parties to gather material for bridges. As soon as this had been done, he sounded the charge again. The detachment sprang forward again, held the bridges and rushed forward over the parapet into the work, capturing the entire garrison, in all two hundred and sixty-five men.

He also speaks of the Fourth Indiana as dashing through the town and scattering a superior force of cavalry, which had just arrived, of which we never heard." *Ib.* p. 364.

It will be seen that in these six official reports of the Federal Officers in command, four state the Fort was taken by assault, while two, Colonel Lampson, of the Fourth and Colonel Harndon, of the First Wisconsin, upon the other side, say that the Fort surrendered.

That the Fort was formally surrendered was known to every Confederate engaged, and every one who has ever written about it state the same thing, and that this surrender did not occur until near sundown, about six o'clock in the afternoon, after eight hours defense, from ten a. m. to six p. m.

This is a simple statement of the facts as I remember them now, after these fifty years, purposely with no mention of heroic acts of individuals, where all acted well, or laudation of the conduct of my comrades as a whole, and without attempt to embellish this story with the graces of rhetoric. The simple story is an eloquent epic in itself.

I trust, however, I may be permitted to quote from a contribution made to commemorate this event, published in the Confederate Veteran of November, 1896, by a participant, W. J. Slater, as big-souled and congenial a spirit as ever lived. I do so as his account concurs, in the material facts of this statement, and possibly because of the kind mention of myself. In referring to the attendants who were there, he says:

"There is Judge McFarland, of Memphis, then a Lieutenant, young and handsome (alas, that was just fifty years ago, dear J. H. when you and I were young), returning to his command (Cheatham's) after a brief furlough, who called on General Tyler to see if he intended to try to hold the Fort. The General said he did, and asked McFarland to stay with him and act as Adjutant for him, as his own was absent. On going into the Fort, McFarland asked permission to burn the houses in its front, suggesting that they were so near that the enemy could use them advantageously in their attack. General Tyler said the people to whom they belonged could not stand the loss, as they were principally beautiful cottage homes, and finally refused to give the order. It was from one of these houses that the sharp shooters fired the ball which killed General Tyler.

"A large fine looking Indian was the first to enter the Fort. He carried an axe and cut down the pole from which floated our banner. On the road home after my parole from prison I met this same Indian, the orderly sergeant of his company, and he told me that General LaGrange had offered a furlough to the one who first entered the Fort, and he secured it."

He also mentions Charlie Locke, one of my company, as above stated, who lost an arm in the Fort. As further tribute to this splendid soldier and honorable man Locke, I add, that he lived an honorable and active life in Memphis until a few winters ago, when there came a covering of ice upon the street, upon which he slipped, and his head struck a curbstone, crushing his skull, and he died from this in a few days.

I also quote what friend Slater writes about General Tyler, as worthy of remembrance and oft repetition, in the same article, in the Confederate Veteran. He says:

"I conclude with a few biographical words in reference to General Robert C. Tyler, born and reared in Baltimore, Md. He was in the Nicaraguan Expedition under Walker in 1859 or 1860, and thence he went to Memphis, Tennessee, where he joined the Fifteenth Tennessee Regiment (Carroll's) as a private in Company "D," was appointed Quartermaster, but went into the fight at Belmont. He was elected Colonel at the re-organization at Corinth. After the battle of Perryville, he was made Provost Marshal General of General Bragg. He was badly wounded at Shiloh. He commanded at Missionary Ridge and was badly wounded there, necessitating the excision of a leg. After this, he was placed in command at West Point. He was a dear friend of mine, and I revere his memory."

I trust I may be further permitted, without imputation of tediousness and too much ego, to tell how General LaGrange treated us after the capture, and especially his courtesy to me. After the surrender in the Fort, I approached him and Col. Fannin, and when the Colonel told him who I was, the General said: "Lieutenant, I am sorry your General was killed, but if you will accept parole, I will take you on my staff until I can dispose of you." I accepted the parole, and the next morning, the General furnished me a horse, and directed me to ride with him. This I did, and for four days I rode with the Brigade from West Point to Macon, Georgia. I was treated with every courtesy and rode at any place with the command between the head and end of the column, and was shown many little attentions by the various officers of the command, and with the greatest courtesy. I remember one day riding along, I got into a warm controversy with one of the officers over the cause of the war, and with the rashness of youth and the vanity of a "little

learning" I talked too much.   The next day one of the Cap-
tains said to me that I must quit such discussions or some
of the men might knock me in the head and lose me.   *I quit.*

Arriving at Macon, before I dismounted, I learned that
General Lee had surrendered, and I read a copy of his farewell address.   I remember even now the shock and temporary feeling of despair which came upon me and lingered
with me during the night.   My horse was then taken.   I
bade General LaGrange farewell, with thanks for his kindness, and was sent to join other prisoners in prison.   The
next morning I was paroled.   I went back to General La
Grange, and he gave me an order for a horse to take me home
to West Tennessee, and I started on my return so soon as I
had my mount.

My soliloquies on this trip were not exactly those of a
soldier that Grady tells about in his Boston talk, who, after
the surrender at Appomatox, and who was trudging along
home, was heard to make this soliloquy to himself:   "Well,
I will go home now and make a crap for my family, and then
if them damn Yankees bother me any more, I will whip them
again."

I never saw or heard of General LaGrange again until
1910.   I was then on a trip to California, and when at Los
Angeles, I learned that General LaGrange was then in command
of the home for Federal Veterans, about a thousand, at that
point.   I sent him my card, and a few evenings after, I had
a note from the General, inviting me to join him at the annual
meeting of the Los Angeles Camp of Federals, then holding
a Banquet at my hotel, the Alexandria.   I went down and
the General met me, and I joined in the Banquet.   They
soon called on me for a speech.   I told of my capture by
General LaGrange and the treatment I received, and my
pleasure at being captured a second time, with other remarks
as to our reconciliation, etc., etc.   Others spoke in the same
strain, and I had quite a pleasant evening.   The General
afterwards spent a day with me at my hotel in Pasadena, all
of which soon occupied a column in the Pasadena papers,
under the heading "Blue and Gray in post-bellum harmony."

I had not at this time, and in fact, not until I began the preparation of this paper, read the official reports which I have quoted above, and General LaGrange and I did not discuss the Fort Tyler event.

In conclusion I again regret I cannot be with you on the 16th, but I wish to congratulate any of the participants (present or living) of the fifty years ago, that they have been spared to this era of a united and prosperous country, and to enjoy the kind and appreciative expressions of their countrymen; and I hope that the Fort Tyler Chapter U. D. C. may be long perpetuated by such noble and patriotic women as now honor and adorn its name.

With great Respect, I am

Very truly

L. B. McFarland.

# THE SWORD COMBAT.

## BETWEEN COL. JOHN GOFF BALLENTINE AND MAJ. CARL SCHAEFER DE BERNSTEIN.

*(Confederate Veteran, January, 1917.)*

BY JUDGE L. B. McFARLAND, MEMPHIS, TENN.

"O for a muse of fire that would ascend
The brightest heaven of invention,
A kingdom for a stage, princes to act,
And monarchs to behold the swelling scene!"

Thus nearly four hundred years ago wrote the Bard of Avon, prologue to a play reciting the deeds of Henry V., erstwhile Prince of Wales, whose combat with Hotspur, Henry Percy, was immortalized by the poet's pen. This combat for all these years since this play was written has had the world for a stage, princes of play to act, and monarchs to behold the swelling scene.

The Bard of Scotland more than a century ago wrote "The Lady of the Lake," describing a sword combat between James Fitz James, King of Scotland, and Roderick Dhu, a rebel Highland chieftain. This romantic story, told in rythmic verse, has charmed the reading world for all these years since its writing. The scene of this combat was at Coilantogle Ford, on the banks of a stream in the highlands of Scotland.

A hundred years or more since the writing of this delightful story an actual combat was staged in a new continent as one of the acts and tragedies of a stupendous war which was an almost identical reproduction of Coilantogle Ford. It was between two officers, Confederate and Federal, fit representatives of the South and North, and it was by a small stream in Tennessee. The Confederate, like Fitz James, was the better swordsman. The Federal, "while less expert, though stronger far, maintained unequal war." In the first, the Highland chief was knightly to his foe, but over-

confident of his prowess in discarding his targe. In the
second, the Southron discarded his pistol, with which he
could have killed his foe with ease and without risk, to accept
the other's challenge to sword combat. The participants in
this tragedy to be related were a brave Federal named Carl
Schaefer de Bernstein and J. G. Ballentine, then a captain
of cavalry under Claiborne and Jackson, fit actors for such
a scene.

Of the Federal, not much could be learned by the writer,
to his regret, as his gallantry on this occasion, to be shown,
merited full recital as to him personally and to his soldierly
deeds.

The Confederate, Captain Ballentine, was of Irish
ancestry. His father, an Irishman, fought with the French
under Bonaparte. He rode with Ney and the Old Guard at
Waterloo in the charge upon the British Guards between
Hougoumont and La Haye Sainte, so thrillingly described
in "Miserables." The disasters of this battle drove Ballen
tine, Sr., to America, and he purchased an estate in Tennes
see near Pulaski. Here his son, John Goff Ballentine, was
born and ripened to manhood. He had all the advantages of the landed youth of the South and acquired the
accomplishments and graces these advantages fostered. He
graduated from Wurtemberg Academy in 1841, from the
University of Nashville in 1845, was a member of the
Harvard Law School Association, attended Livingston Law
School of New York, and was practicing his profession of law
at Memphis when the war came. In addition to these accomplishments, all outdoor sports and manly exercise were cultivated. His father, expert with a sword himself, taught
him from his youth up all the arts of fencing and made him
also an accomplished swordsman. ·At the time of his enlistment he was about five feet nine inches in height, slender,
but with muscle and nerve of steel and the activity of an
athlete. He delighted in fine apparel, wore his dark-brown
hair long, and was a handsome and picturesque figure, re-
calling knights of the Crusades, subjects of troubadour songs
and minstrel lays, or suggesting cavaliers of the Charles-the-
First age, and yet he was no carpet knight,

"Whose best boast was to wear
A braid of some fair lady's hair."

but had the strong virtues of virile manhood that commanded respect and made him a soldier, a colonel and in civil life a member of Congress for years. He was a splendid horseman, in battle always leading his men with dash, courage, and abandon.

With this foreword, the writer gives now the facts as to this combat in simple recital, leaving for some future "mute inglorious Milton," some Bard of Avon, or Scottish poet to give the incident the proper setting.

In May, 1862, Colonel Claiborne, in command of two Confederate regiments, the 6th and 7th Tennessee Cavalry, determined to attack a Federal cavalry force, under Maj. Carl Schaefer de Bernstein and Capt. W. A. Hall and Henry Van Minden, then near Dresden, Tenn. Overtaking them on the 5th of May at Lockridge Mill, on the south fork of the Obion River, an attack was made at once by five companies of Claiborne's men under Acting Field Officer Captain Ballentine. This attack soon routed the enemy, who retreated in disorder, but individually fighting gallantly when overtaken; and for ten miles the pursuit and melee continued, resulting in many hand-to-hand conflicts. In his official report of this fight Colonel Claiborne states as follows: "Captain Ballentine was most conspicuous of all for his gallant bearing and use of his saber and pistol. He fired upon and mortally wounded Maj. Carl Schaefer de Bernstein. He engaged in a saber hand-to-hand combat with a brave fellow named Hoffman, who several times pierced the Captain's coat with his saber, but was finally forced to yield. Captain Ballentine also received blows by a carbine and was seriously bruised."

It will be seen that Colonel Claiborne says it was Schaefer de Bernstein who was mortally wounded and that it was with Hoffman he engaged in sword combat. The other officers likewise agree that it was Schaefer who was mortally wounded, and Colonel Ballentine stated to the writer that it was with him the sword combat took place. The official reports were properly only meager statements of the

action, and this paper is written to give the details and present
in fuller light the gallantry and chivalry of Colonel Ballentine
on this occasion as a fit meed to valor due.  These details
the writer had soon after the war from Lieutenant Somerville, of Ballentine's command, a participant in this fight and
in part a witness to the fight itself, and subsequently from
Colonel Ballentine himself a few years before his death, told
reluctantly and after much persuasion.

These details, as now recalled, are that in the pursuit of
the Federals, who had been badly scattered, Captain Ballentine, somewhat in advance of his men, was pursuing a Fed
eral officer who was covering the retreat of his men, and he
(Ballentine), being better mounted, was gaining upon the
Federal.  This officer, Major Schaefer, gallantly covering
the retreat of his men, crossed the bridge spanning the south
fork of Obion River and, like Leonidas at Therymopylæ,
stopped to defend its passage.  Captain Ballentine, in the
lead of his men, came dashing down the road to the bridge
and without halting charged across, pistol in hand, to attack
his opponent.  As he was crossing the bridge his opponent
fired several times at him, emptying his pistol, but without
effect, while Ballentine reserved his fire for closer quarters.
When within a few feet of his opponent, with his pistol
within "six feet" (said Colonel Ballentine) and about to fire,
Major Schaefer suddenly lowered his pistol, exclaiming, "My
pistol is empty; draw your sword," drawing his own sword
at the same time.

This appealed to all the chivalric sentiment of Ballentine's nature.  Here was the opportunity his ardent spirit had
longed for come at last to try his arm and sword and test
his father's teaching.  He stopped his horse on his haunches,
replaced his pistol in his holster, and drew his saber, not a
heavy one like his opponent's, but much lighter and shorter,
though of tried temper.  They met.  Their swords flashed
and crossed.  They fought, each putting in play all the force
and skill he had, soon intensified by early knowledge of the
skill of opponent and seriousness of the conflict.  Ballentine
soon discovered that his opponent was the stouter of the two

and his saber longer and heavier; but Ballentine was the better mounted of the two, and it was his own skill and coolness and horsemanship, with the mettle and activity of his thoroughbred, that must overcome the odds against him. They were now hand to hand, sword to sword, parrying and striking, and then as the impetus of their charges passed each the other, both would wheel and charge again and thrust and guard. Many attacks like these were renewed without wound until the brave Federal and good swordsman brought to play his advantage of weight of self and blade, and in the next charge, in the moment of contact, he with both hands delivered a descending blow with his heavy blade. This was met by proper guard, and saber met saber; but weight and strength broke through, and the blade descending upon the Captain's head cut a deep gash, from which the blood ran down his face and in his eyes.

Even this did not daunt his courage or confidence. The impetus of this charge carried them apart again, and in the interval of vault and charge the Southron brought to play the speed and strength of his horse and with sword and spur drove his horse against the opposite steed, literally riding both down, and as the rider reeled the Southron pierced him through. He fell to the ground insensible and mortally wounded, and none too soon, for almost at the same instant exertion and wound had done their work on the Southron and with him "reeled soul and sense, reeled brain and eye," and he too fell from his horse insensible.

Fortunately, some of Ballentine's men came up at this instant and ministered as they could to the combatants, and upon returning consciousness of both they were placed in a country cart together and taken to the nearest town, Dresden, and given rooms and attention in the same house. Captain Ballentine soon recovered and resumed his command. The brave Schaefer died that night, but before he died he requested that his victor, of whom he spoke with praise of both his gallantry and his generosity, should have his horse, pistol, and sword as lawful spoil of war.

It was said by Burke that the age of chivalry is no more. Had he lived and been familiar with the thousands of incidents of individual heroism that characterized our four years' conflict, had he witnessed the scene just described and seen Captain Ballentine, challenged as he was, with his opponent enemy absolutely at his mercy, relinquish his own advantage, give his enemy his life, and fight him upon equal terms, Burke would have said: "The age of chivalry has come again, and knighthood is in flower."

It is proper to add that the saber and pistol given to Ballentine in this combat came near proving fatal to the victor, for years after a fire destroyed the Ballentine home. The Colonel ran to the upper room, then in flames, where these were stored, but, being blinded and nearly overcome, had to be dragged from his peril, and the pistol and sword were destroyed.

# FIRST TO RE ENLIST FOR THE WAR.

*(From Confederate Veteran, September, 1916.)*

The Confederate Veteran is and has been doing great service. It not only gives pleasure to the Veterans them selves and the Sons and their families, brightening many a home, but is also the repository of valuable historic material that is being and will be woven into permanent history, correcting error, establishing truth, perpetuating individual worth and national honor as exemplified by the South. This we regard as the Veteran's broad field of labor and noble work. Its active Spirit is and has been its love of the South, and this is the vital Soul that perpetuates its existence. We feel there is a corresponding duty upon every participant in the stirring days of '61 and '65 to contribute each his wealth or mite of facts aiding in the establishment of the truths of history. If the rivulets run not to the river and the river to the ocean, then woe to the world.

This prelude, together with the sense of duty to my comrades of my old regiment, is my apology for asking leave to print the following:

The question of which regiment of the army of Tennessee was the first to re-enlist for the War, has been much discussed. One general order was issued and a number of articles have heretofore appeared in the Veteran on this subject, but so far no mention has been made in the Veteran of the regiment and brigade to which I belong, or its claim to the honor of being the first to re-enlist.

On the 1st day of March, 1864, Hon. Ben E. Hill made a speech at LaGrange, Ga., giving credit to Bates' brigade as being the first to enlist. On June 1st, 1864, Gen. Joseph E. Johnston promulgated the following order:

"I have received official notice that Strahl's Brigade, Army of Tennessee, has followed the example of Vaughn's and re-enlisted for the war and that this movement was started by the 154th Tennessee Regiment of the latter brigade, which has the honor of inaugurating this plan." ("Official Records.")—Confederate Veteran, July, 1916, page 291.

There appears in the Veteran of                        on page 171 an article on this subject from Col. William B. Pickett, a noble, gallant officer, still living, attached at the time to the staff of Gen. Hardee, to whose corps Gen. Cheatham's Division in which the movement is agreed to have started is assigned.  He says:

"My distinct recollection is that this movement was started in Vaughn's Tennessee Brigade of Cheatham's Division, Hardee's Corps.  If it started by regiments, it commenced in the consolidated One Hundred and Fifty-Fourth Tennessee and the Fourth Tennessee."

Now the purpose of this article is not to question the correctness of the facts as stated in Gen. Johnston's order, nor the recollection of Col. Pickett as quoted above.  That the number was *started* by the 154th Tennessee Regiment Vaughn's Brigade, and its example was followed by Strahl's Brigade.  But the purpose of this article is to claim for the 6th and 9th Tennessee Infantry consolidated Cheatham's Division, the credit of being the first to actually re-enlist. Col. Pickett further adds in this article:

"There should be no difficulty at getting at the facts of this matter, as there must be many officers and soldiers of Cheatham's Division still living who are cognizant of the facts."

He also adds:

"This matter should be thoroughly ventilated now that it is up is my excuse for going so much into detail.  Certainly no event in her history confers higher honor, under all the circumstances, upon Tennessee and Tennessee troops.  There should be erected in the capitol grounds at Nashville a monument dedicated to 'Tennessee Valor,' and inscribed on it should be a copy of the first resolution passed for 'reenlistment,' and below it the names of the Tennessee commands that adopted it in regular order."

Col. Pickett, in the same article, suggests, as a means of best determining this question, the evidence of officers and soldiers on Gen. Cheatham's division cognizant of the facts, and by reference to the newspapers of that period, mentioning the Appeal. These are but the sources, contemporary statement from which the law and universal experience history establishes truth.

To bring the evidence I now submit, within these suggestions and under these recognized rules of evidence, that I was an officer in the 9th Tennessee Infantry, made Sergeant Major of my regiment at Shiloh, and subsequently made Lieutenant of the company, and acted as aid on Gen. Maney's staff, and was at Dalton, Ga., and I sometimes, verifying the Latin lines *"Docti Scribimus, indoctigue."* translated by Pope thus: "Those who can't write and those who can, All rhyme and scrawl and scribble to a man"; wrote articles about current army happenings, writing them under my Byronic *nom de plume* "Conrad," and the article I quote below was published at the time in the Appeal, a copy of which was cut out and carried in my knapsack the balance of the war, and I have the same now.

"A CORRECTION.

Dalton, Ga., March 22, 1864.

Editors Appeal: In your report today of the speech of the Hon. B. H. Hill, delivered at LaGrange, Ga., on the 1st of March, the following passage occurs: 'Noble Tennessee! foremost among the brave—Bates' Brigade to reenlist.' Now, while I appreciate the compliment paid to Tennessee and her sons; while I welcome it as indicative of the feelings of kindness which Georgians exercise towards our homeless wanderers, and while I do not wish to appear as criticizing any part of the noble Senator's speech, or his information upon this subject of re-enlistment, still I do wish to see an erroneous opinion, now wide-spread, corrected—that is, that of Bates' brigade being the foremost of Tennesseeans to reenlist.

The facts of the case are these, as will be shown by reference to the back numbers of the Appeal: Bates' brigade was not the first to re-enlist. The 154th Tennessee, of Vaughn's brigade, claims that distinguished honor, and with considerable justice too, as this was the first to receive the thanks of our Congress for so doing. Yet they even were not the *first to re-enlist*. That honor is claimed by the 6th and 9th Tennessee regiments of Maney's brigade. It is true that a week anterior to the actual re-enlistment of the 6th and 9th, the 154th unanimously passed resolutions declaring their willingness to serve through the war, yet, still, they did not so obligate themselves in a manner to be considered binding. This the 6th and 9th did do, by marching almost *en masse*, to the colonel's quarters, unattended by a single officer, and demanding to be mustered in for the war, which was done.

This act of patriotism so timely begun by the 154th and so happily executed by the 6th and 9th Tennessee, aroused at once that spirit of generous rivalry which has ever characterized the brigades of Cheatham's division, and they hastened to declare, by regiments, their determination of eternal resistance. Vaughn's whole brigade and a majority of Cheatham's remaining brigades had re-enlisted before the electric spark had caught in Bates' brigade. These are facts substantiated by the resolutions passed by the different regiments, and published in the Appeal at the time."

Again, Prof. H. C. Irby, now living at Jackson, Tenn., and for years prominent in the faculty of West Tennessee University, was captain of Company D, 6th and 9th Tennessee Regiment consolidated. He was dangerously wounded at Perryville in the charge of his regiment on the battery at Jackson, which we took, and the guns of which did noble service under Capt. Turner, until the end of the war.

In a sketch prepared by him of the 9th Tennessee Infantry for Lindsley's Military Annals, published 1886, will be found, page 278, the following:

"During the time we were in winter-quarters at Dalton an event occurred which justly gives to Tennessee a new title to be called the 'Volunteer State.' The time for which most of the troops had been enlisted would soon expire. The question was much discussed: What shall be done to prevent a depletion of the army? The 'Gordian-knot' was cut by an action of the consolidated Sixth and Ninth regiments, led by Co. A, of the Sixth. Every man volunteered to reenlist. This example was at once followed by other regiments, until the whole army was "in for the war.' "

Fortunately, Col. George C. Porter, then colonel of the regiment, and Major J. A. Wilder, then major, and both at Dalton, Ga., both gallant officers and well known, are still alive, and to them I have submitted the foregoing, and they fully concur in the facts as given, Colonel Porter, in addition, calls my attention to the fact that subsequent to Colonel Pickett's article in the Veteran, quoted above, in a sketch of General Hardee, now in the Tennessee Historical Association, he (Colonel Pickett) credits Company A, 6th Tennessee, with starting this movement and files as an appendix to this sketch a statement from E. M. Seymour, orderly sergeant of this company, well known to me as one of the bravest soldiers and best of men, giving the facts as to actual reenlistment sub-•tantially as set out in the foregoing.

In order to verify the correctness of my statement above, and adopting the suggestion of Colonel Pickett, I have examined the files of the Appeal from December, 1893, to April, 1894, and find the following: "In the Appeal of January 18, 1864, appears an article from Col. M. Magevney, colonel of the 154th Tennessee, sending resolutions passed by his regiment on the 14th of January, saying: 'We are prepared to concur in any legislation that Congress may devise for the better organization of the army. * * * And that we tender our services to the country as long as its exigencies need them.' "

In the issue of January 20, 1864, appear resolutions as passed on the 15th of January by Strahl's Brigade, to the same effect as those of the 154th Regiment, "tendering our services." This issue also shows that the 13th Tennessee passed similar resolutions on the same date. In the issue of January 28 appears an article from a correspondent, signed "Old Aven," which says: "While at Dalton on the 22d of January I visited the 6th and 9th Tennessee Regiment, and while there the regiment marched to the colonel's headquarters and notified this officer that they were ready to enlist. . . . While other regiments, in common with this, have expressed an intention in the form of resolutions of tendering their services to the government until peace shall have been declared, the meed of praise is justly due to this regiment for being the first to renew again upon the altar of their country their determination to be free." This writer, name unknown, further described in detail the actual ceremony of reenlistment. It was Sunday evening. The companies came in succession and there in the moonlight bared and bowed their heads and were sworn by the colonel to serve until peace was attained, thus making the solemn scene of this holy day a religious ceremony.

The writer further says the first company that was sworn in was Company A, Capt. R. C. Williamson, and the second Company D, Capt. J. B. Locke. Company A was composed, as consolidated, of two companies from the 6th Tennessee, and Company D was composed of Company A, of which I was an officer, and Company D of the 9th Tennessee. In this issue of the 27th of January an editorial notices this re enlistment of the 6th and 9th Tennessee "without resolutions" and says: "These regiments were the first brigade under Brigadier General (now Major General) Cheatham and have shared whatever glory that may attach to his in the above career. They are composed of West Tennesseans exclusively and are commanded by Col. George C. Porter, than whom a more gallant and efficient officer is rarely found."

I submit the foregoing evidence of living participants and uncontradicted contemporary statements to be conclusive of what regiment of the Western Army was "the first to re-enlist."

# CONGRESSIONAL RECORD U. S.

### ADDRESS BY JUDGE L. B. McFARLAND AT REUNION OF UNITED CONFEDERATE VETERANS, MACON, GA., MAY 8, 1912.

May 25, 1912.

Mr. McKellar said:

Mr. Speaker: On May 12 the House held memorial exercises in honor of my predecessor from Memphis, the late Gen. George W. Gordon. Only a few days before, Judge L. B. McFarland, a distinguished and eloquent lawyer of Memphis and ex-Confederate soldier, and a lifelong friend of Gen. Gordon, delivered an able and beautiful address upon the life and character of Gen. Gordon before the annual reunion of ex-Confederate veterans at Macon, Ga., and it is so beautiful and fitting a tribute that I ask unanimous consent that it may be printed in the Record as a part of my remarks and included as one of the memorial addresses of this House upon the life and character of my distinguished predecessor. It is especially fitting that this address should have a place in the Record, because it contains an unfinished and hitherto unpublished farewell address of Gen. Gordon to his old comrades in arms.

The address is as follows:

Beloved commander and comrades, when delegated by our commander in chief to deliver on this occasion a memorial of the life and character of your late commander in chief, Gen. George W. Gordon, I hesitated to attempt compliance, fearing that my great admiration for the subject, born from years of intimate association, would tempt to adulation, and, on the other hand, my incapacity to speak fittingly of a character so noble, and a life so full of usefulness, self-sacrifice, and noble deeds, gave me pause. I felt the deeds of such a man should not be feebly uttered, but I took the delegation to be a command and an honor, and the opportunity to perpetuate in the records of this association a tribute to a dead friend and brother could not be disregarded.

George W. Gordon was born on the 5th day of October, 1836, in Giles County, Tenn. He was the son of Andrew Gordon, a native of Tennessee, and Eliza K. Gordon, Virginian born. This county—one of the blue-grass region of Tennessee—was one of the most fertile and fairest of the land, its people educated, refined and prosperous to a high degree. He was reared there and in Mississippi and also Texas, he having spent part of his youth in each. He graduated at the Western Military Institute, at Nashville, then the West Point of the South, and was thus fitted for the performance of arms. He first made civil engineering his occupation, and served in that field from 1859 to 1861, and until Tennessee seceded from the Union and called her sons to arms. He enlisted at once and was made drillmaster of the afterwards famous Eleventh Tennessee Infantry, whose first colonel was Col. J. E. Raines, afterwards Gen. Raines, who fell in a desperate conflict at Murfreesboro. Gordon was soon made captain of his company, and then lieutenant colonel and then colonel of his regiment, and in 1864 was made brigadier general.

At the close of the war he studied law and was early elected attorney general of one of the criminal courts of Shelby County, Tenn., and served the State ably and well. He was then appointed a railroad commissioner for the State, and served until 1885, when, upon the election of Mr. Cleveland, he received an appointment in the Department of the Interior, and was assigned to duty in charge of an Indian agency amid the mountains of Arizona and Nevada. He was eminently fitted for this particular post, feeding, educating, and controlling these children of nature and wards of the Government, and these duties and opportunities were congenial to the habits of his then lonely life and his intense love of nature.

It required that he take, alone and unattended, long trips amid the solitudes and vastnesses of the mountains, now wandering through beautiful meadows where the dun deer fed and the grizzly roamed, and then high above the clouds, threading the narrow path that wound around seemingly bottomless precipices; often overtaken by storm, he reveled in the grandeur of nature's supremest effort—saw the lightning flash and heard the thunders roll, when—

"Far along—
From peak to peak, the rattling crags
Among, leaps the live thunder."

And then at night, his horse tethered near, he made his lonely bivouac under the clear heavens and near the clear stars, and felt himself as did Moses, communing with the God of all these wondrous works. To him this was not solitude—

" 'Twas but to hold converse with nature's charms and view her stores unrolled."

His term of office expired, he returned to Memphis, and was soon elected superintendent of the Memphis city schools, which office he held until March, 1907, when he was elected to Congress. The growth and efficiency of the public-school system of Memphis during these years became a monument to his zeal, intelligence, and devotion to his work, and the spread of general education and intelligence signaled his beneficent influence upon the youthful thousands under his superintendence, while the gratitude and devotion of teachers and scholars was afterwards demonstrated by their activity and influence in his several candidacies for Congress. He had raised an army of constitutents for any office in the gift of his people. He was twice elected to Congress—in 1908, and reelected in 1910—by overwhelming majorities given by an appreciative constituency, where he served with the same zeal, fidelity, and devotion he gave any duty of life.

Gen. Gordon was married twice. While attorney general of Shelby County, in 1876, he married Miss Ora Paine. Their bridal trip was to Niagara Falls. I met them there. She a lovely young woman in all the bloom and beauty of youth. He noble in manly bearing—his brow bound with the oak of his many battles; and with them love was dear and life was sweet, and their future horizon seemed spanned with the golden bow of promise. They went to New York. In a

few weeks she was dead.   Bridal carols turned to funeral
dolors; the orange wreath decked her bier; and instead of the
joyous wedding march was heard the sad words of the ritual,
"He cometh up and is cut down like a flower.   Earth to
earth—dust to dust."   He was alone and desolate.

In 1899 he was fortunate in finding a companion of congenial culture and taste in Miss Minnie Hannah, of Memphis,
with whom he was married, who thence shared the honors
showered upon him by a grateful constituency, and graced his
every station.   She survives him to remember with pride that
she was the wife of a soldier, a gentleman, and your commander in chief.

The limits of this occasion will permit only a suggestion
of his services as a soldier, his adventures, and his distinguished gallantry on every field.   Captured early in 1862,
he was a prisoner for 10 days and then exchanged.   Desperately wounded at Murfreesboro in one of the bloodiest
struggles of that field, he was left on the retreat and again
became a prisoner, and on recovery, after long suffering, was
held in prison at Camp Chase and then Fort Delaware, suffering the horrors of those hells until May, 1863, when he
was again exchanged and returned to the command of his
regiment, then in Pres Smith's brigade, Cheatham's division.
Then followed Chickamauga, Missionary Ridge; then the
campaign from Dalton to Jonesboro, 121 days under fire,
including the conflicts of Resaca, Calhoun, New Hope
Church, and Kenesaw Mountain.   With his regiment he held
part of the celebrated Dead Angle.   He was made brigadier
general at that time, and then the youngest of brigadier generals, he first led his brigade at Peachtree Creek, then on the
22d day of July, at Jonesboro.   After came the disastrous
campaign into Tennessee, and, perhaps, the most useless battle
and bloodiest slaughter of the war—Franklin.

Gen. Gordon led his brigade in the desperate charge up
to and over the breastworks "into the very jaws of hell,"
when he was captured.

There is an interesting incident connected with this
charge and capture of Gordon.   Earlier in the war Gordon

had permitted his hair to grow longer than military rules sanctioned, and Gen. Cheatham, in sending him an order one day, added jocularly to his adjutant: "Ingram, tell GORDON to cut off that hair." Ingram delivered his orders, adding, as directed, the supplement. GORDON replied· "Tell Gen. Cheatham I will carry out his military order, but tell him it is none of his business how I wear my hair."

It became somewhat a matter of jest with Cheatham, who was devoted to GORDON, and of pride with GORDON, who was equally devoted to Cheatham, to wear his hair long. When Cheatham ordered the charge at Franklin, he sent word to GORDON to go over the works if he had to be pulled over by his hair. After his capture, when leaving with his captors, he left word with a citizen to tell Gen. Cheatham "GORDON had gone over the works, and was not pulled over by his hair, either."

During the terrible epidemic of yellow fever in Memphis in 1873, he was one of a heroic band that remained, and for many dark days of suffering and death preserved order, ministered to the sick, and buried the dead, displaying self-sacrifice and heroism greater than all the boasted mastery of arms.

He was, after the war, a Confederate in heart and soul and purse. No appeal for help coming from the aged or crippled Confederates, though often pretended nobility was made a plea of pity, was ever disregarded. Gen. GORDON was closely affiliated with Confederate organizations, and successively made commander of his camp and bivouac at Memphis, president of the Confederate Historical Association, Memphis (oldest of the Confederate organs), and of which Mr. Davis himself was a member; president of the State Association of Confederate Bivouacs; major general commander Tennessee Division, United Confederate Veterans; commander of the Department of the Army of Tennessee, United Confederate Veterans; and, crowning all, commander in chief of United Confederate Veterans.

His devotion to his comrades in arms and his duties in this high office at your last reunion at Little Rock hastened his death, and at Memphis, Tenn., he died on the 9th of August, 1911.

His funeral cortege was a weeping city; his dirge the farewell shot by his beloved comrades, Company A, United Confederate Veterans, over the grave of the hero we buried —and our commander in chief departed to return nevermore.

These are in brief the prominent facts of his life, but they naturally suggest inquiry from whence sprung such nobleness of character, such high ideals of duty, and such ability of performance.

The power of heredity, and the influence of climate, food, and soils upon the character of men is an essential thesis of science. These, with the impress of an age's morality, the advantages of education and fortune, the civilization of a particular era, shape and mold men to physical and intellectual worth and greatness. It is also equally well established that the tendency is to harmony of human types along east and west isothermal lines. That, unless marked topographical and race differentiation intervene, the same characteristics will mark the men of Carolina that appear in the men of Texas. These elements, then, of heredity, climate, soil, and social economy had united in the growth of a race of young men in the South, from Maryland to Florida, and westward to the Rio Grande, immediately preceding the Civil War, whose superior, physically, intellectually, and morally, the world had never seen. I know that some foreign and northern writers, political economists, and pseudophilosophers assert that religious freedom was the motive of the northern settlement, while greed of gold was that which populated Virginia and the Carolinas, and from this argue a nobler race of men for the North.

Mr. Draper says:

"The settlement of the South was inspired by material interests; that of the North by ideas. * * * Aristocratic influence was the motive power of southern immigration; it sought material profit in tobacco and land speculation."

It is not appropriate here and now to attempt comparison of sections nor depreciate the worth and greatness of any portion of our people. We only assert that the early settlers of the South, the ancestors of our southern youth, brought with them the physical, mental, and moral characteristics of a high order of humanity and civilization. They brought with them lofty ideals of the rights of man and man's relation to God. In the face of obstacles that would have deterred a less hardy race, they subdued a wilderness, conquered the warlike inhabitants, and assisted in the establishment of an empire. They rebelled against the parental tyranny of England, and the sons of Hampden and Sydney successfully fought the first revolution. Their sons and daughters then addressed themselves to the extension of this territory, the perfection of constitutional government, and the upbuilding of their private and family fortunes. The South "blossomed one day and bore fruit the next." That they had succeeded beyond the dreams of Raleigh or the ambition of Baltimore, the population, the wealth, and the culture of the South in 1861 attest.

I wish the time and the occasion would permit me to sketch the condition of the South at this period; its material wealth, its political economy, its social organization, the influence of slavery upon this people, and particularly the habits of its young men. Whatever may have been the influence of slavery upon the material growth of the South, and what ever may have been its evils, there was certainly a compensating effect in the production of a society the highest and most delightful.

Mr. Burke, in his celebrated oration on Conciliation with America, one of the English classics, in speaking of the love of liberty in America, says:

"In Virginia and the Carolinas they had a vast multitude of slaves. Where this is the case in any part of the world, those who are free are by far the most proud and jealous of their freedom. Freedom is to them not only an enjoyment but a kind of rank and privilege."

The well-to-do, including slave-owning, society of the South had no superior. It was an aristocracy that fostered and cultivated the noblest sentiments of humanity—culture, independence, courage, and knightly courtesy among men;

grace, beauty and virtue among its women. Its hospitality was unbounded. The stately homes of the James, the homes and the plantations of the whole South, were scenes of elegant hospitality. Roman riches and the Roman villas and gardens of the days of Cicero, Atticus, and Lucullus were not more famed for elegant hospitality. The lives of the young men were but a training in all manly arts, all noble endeavor. All outdoor sports and manly exercise were theirs. They delighted in horses and rode like centaurs. The ear and eye, accustomed to hunt and chase, could detect the rustle of a leaf and spy ptarmigan in snow. They fished with skill and swam like Leander. These manly exercises, with generous food and genial but hardy climate, resulted in fine physical perfection. They were, as a class, a handsome race of men. They were graduates of the best schools, and many of them foreign alumni. The first American to graduate in a foreign university was a Virginian. While born and trained as masters, the parental authority of the race taught them obedience and restraint. Their belief in the rights of man did not teach them socialism, nor independence of thought and workship in religion, nor skepticism of the great truths of Christianity. They were taught that "valor was the chiefest virtue, and most dignified the haver." They were near enough to the frontier life of their fathers and to the Revolution to catch, at the fireside, stories of the endurance, the skill, and the bravery of those who fought Indians—of how Washington commanded and Marion rode. Kings Mountain and Yorktown were to them places of pilgrimage—the graves of the heroes of the Revolution were around them. They had themselves declaimed in every schoolhouse from Richmond to Austin the fiery and patriotic words of Patrick Henry.

It was not wonderful then, that when the South was to be invaded—by whom they did not care, for what they did not stop to ask—her youth poured out from every schoolhouse, college, and university at the first call.

The log school houses and colleges of the South—Lebanon, LaGrange, Chapel Hill, Lexington, Nashville, and hundreds of others—each gave their all of youth. It was a goodly sight to see these handsome boys and young men, full of courage, ardor, and ambition, come and offer themselves, their lives, and their fortunes to their beloved land.

How well they redeemed the offer cannot be told. Their endurance in the cold and weary marches with Jackson in the valley, with Bragg in Kentucky; their courage at Manassas, Richmond, and Chickamauga, all attest that this heredity, climate, and other influences had made a race of heroes. The story of Mars Chan is a true epic of these days.

In this outline we have but suggested the genius and pictured the character, the prowess, and the performances of Gen. GORDON.

But it is of him as a man that I would fain dwell longest and most lovingly.

In his early manhood he was a picture of manly grace and bearing. Some 5 feet 8½ inches in height, weighing some 140 pounds, erect and lithe—a face symmetrical in features, but without a trace of effeminacy, with firmness and decision written in every line. His eyes were dark, quickly melting to tenderness at another's woes, but on occasions flashing with the suppressed lightning of passion. His brown hair, while a soldier, unwittingly neglected, would sometimes hang in golden brown to his shoulders, suggesting the cavalier of the Charles the First age.

A gallant and distinguished officer writes of him as he then appeared at the head of his brigade as—

"The long, curly-haired, young brigadier from Tennessee, of dashing field qualities, and handsome personal appearance."

He was a splendid horseman, witching the world with noble horsemanship. Mounted and leading his men to battle he was a picture for troubadour song. It was thus he rode in many a conflict. The romance and the history and song of southern literature are justly full of the pictures of Stuart and Ashby and Forrest, as they rode in battle, but had GORDON been a cavalryman, with their opportunities for sin-

gle combat and individual display, his name would have linked
with theirs.

He was an earnest man. To whatever he was called he
devoted himself earnestly and seriously. To him life was
earnest—life was real. He knew little of society—was too
much of a monologist, with hobbies, to be entertaining in a
drawing room, talked only occasionally and always with force.
He was fond of books and loved the beautiful in everything;
devoted to music, and in his early years, like our Bob, played
the violin well.

One of the chief characteristics of his life was his sense
of and devotion to duty. Whatever he thought it was his
duty to do he did, like Luther, "though devils block his way."

Another characteristic was his high sense of honor, or
rather his sensitiveness to honor. Other men might do things
and feel no wrong, but from the same acts he would instinc-
tively and intuitively shrink.

His was a soul—
"To whom dishonor's shadow is a substance
More terrible than death here and hereafter,
And who though proof against all blandishments
Of pleasure and all pangs of pain, are feeble,
When the proud name on which they pinnacled,
Their fame is breathed on."

And woe to the man or men who breathed upon the
bright escutcheon of his honor.

His attainments were scholarly, and as a public speaker
he was animated, forceful, and classic. He was much in
demand, and was ready on all Confederate occasions and delighted at every opportunity for commemorating the virtues
and gallantry of Confederates. His eulogy on the life and
services of the great commander, Joseph E. Johnston, delivered to an immense audience in Memphis, was a masterpiece
of power and pathos, and a classic oration.

Another of his chiefest virtues was his earnest and constant devotion to his friends. To those virtues of valor and

gentleness, of sense of duty and practice of virtue, add truth and honesty, and we have said it all. No wonder that living he was loved by all, and dying his obsequies were an affectionate outpouring of a whole people. All felt that this earth that bears him dead bears not alive so true a gentleman.

With him, as is often the case, death brought a retrospect of the dearest aims and strongest emotions of his life, and as the fluttering pulse presaged the coming end he was upon the battle field among his men again. The serried rank, the charging squadron, the waving banners, the rattle of musketry, the roar of cannon, and all the pride, pomp, and cir cumstance of the big war were his again, and his last words were, "Send other couriers; those may be killed."

But, comrades, I wish to add in conclusion that his chiefest aim in life was to vindicate the justness of the Confederate cause and to assist in the perpetuation of the honor and glory of the Confederate soldier. His chiefest ambition was to be your commander, and his love and devotion to you his intensest emotion. The chief purpose of my coming before you today was to bring you a message from him. His last thoughts were of you.

While gradually sinking to the Great Beyond his thoughts were with you, and he wrote you a last farewell, and that I will read to you from his own pencil:

*"To the Federation of United Confederate Veterans, comrades and countrymen:*

"About to die, I salute you, and in bidding you a final farewell I desire once more to make my profoundest acknowledgments and to express my heartfelt gratitude to you for the many manifestations of your partiality and devotion, evidenced by the many honors that you have conferred upon me, and more especially for the last profound and exalted distinction with which you have crowned me—that of making me your commander in chief. I esteem this last expression of your regard and consideration a grander and more glorious distinction than all of the combined public plaudits, achievements, decorations, and honors of my entire life, and for which I would express my thanks and appreciation from the grave. What patriotic glory can equal that of being the commander in chief of the surviving and venerable fragments of those brave and heroic Confederate armies who for four trying and perilous years maintained their cause against odds of more than four to one, and who fought battles and won victories when barefooted, ragged, and hungry, and who at last were overpowered more by the preponderance of numbers and resources than by courage and prowess—more by famine than by fighting * * *"

This last farewell to you was never finished.

Here, my comrades, the pulse of life throbbed low; his feeble hand could write no more, and in a few days his noble spirit winged its flight to join again, we hope, his comrades gone before, all to await our speedy coming in the great reunion hereafter.

## ELLEN SAUNDERS McFARLAND.

### (THE LITTLE REBEL.)

Extracts relating to the Civil War from the journal of Ellen Virginia, youngest child of Col. James E. Saunders of Courtland, Ala., beginning in 1862, when she was but 14 years of age. (She married in 1872, Judge L. B. McFarland, of Memphis, Tenn.)

*(Montgomery Advertiser, July 13, 1902.)*

Rocky Hill, near Courtland, Ala.
September 26, 1862.

It has been many a day since last I wrote in my journal, but now I will begin anew. My eldest brother, Robert, is now with the Virginia Army, and on General Cook's staff. My brother, Dudley, is a surgeon in the army of Chattanooga. My youngest brother, Lawrence, is nearly 17. I had not yet told you, my journal, of my father's severe wounding in the battle of Murfreesboro, Tenn. (Sunday, July 13th, 1862), while as aid-de-camp to Gen. N. B. Forrest, he was leading his men in a charge on the Court House; he rode off a short distance and dismounting staggered into a little cottage (though shot entirely through the right chest) and there fell upon a pallet where some poor children were at play. In falling his Maynard Rifle (which he still carried) further injured his shattered rib. While lying there an officer came to him, and he, supposing himself dying, gave him some messages and also his watch to send home. The officer, stepping out of the gate, was instantly killed, and his pockets rifled by the Yankees. In the meanwhile Dr. Wendel reached my father just in time, since he was suffocating and strangling with the blood. He was permitted to remain at the residence of Colonel Sedbeth's, where he was kindly nursed by citizens until the Confederates again captured Murfreesboro, and he was released.

My cousin, Washington Foster, and his friend, Edward O'Neal, of Florence, were here to-day. Wash has joined a company for three years "not to come home unless brought there wounded or dead," he says. He is a high-minded boy and I hope will be promoted. His brother, Jack Foster, has also enlisted. Mr. O'Neal is pleasant, handsome and considered very bright by every one. Mary Wheatley and I are very busy. Sister Kate (Mrs. Dr. Saunders), hears our lessons and conducts our course of reading.

### October 5th—Sunday—

It is a family custom with us to have a kind of Sunday School, while unable to go to Church. The Bible and a sermon are read and a favorite old hymn sung, and perhaps a sacred poem recited by some of us. And now while I write the voices of the family group come up to me in the song. How thankful am I that my father is spared to us! I think I love him more than anything on earth. What would life be to me without him, so refined and intellectual, and so gentle! I wish I loved to read my Bible, for it is certainly my duty. Mary says she is glad it is Sunday for we do not have any lessons. My brother Lawrence has gone with some military dispatches to a camp near Iuka, Miss. Col. Thomas Foster, a Congressman, uncle-in-law of mine, is expected here to-morrow. He is just returning from Richmond, Va., where the Confederate Congress is held.

### October 6th—

Heigho! I have the blues! Lawrie has not returned, nor Uncle Tom Foster arrived. To-night the news reached us of a great victory gamed by Gen. Stirling Price at Corinth, Miss. Three cheers for the dear Confederates! I do pray the Southern banners may float victorious in the North! They say General Bragg has taken Louisville. Stonewall Jackson and his brave men are in "Maryland, My Maryland." The Mobile Cadets were the first to cross the Potomac, and when they were all over, General Jackson at the head of his troops, prayed "that the chains of Maryland might soon be riven, and the Confederate flag shield her evermore from the touch of the despot." And the soldiers knelt and kissed the soil of Maryland, brave Maryland!

October 13th—

On the 11th Mary Wheatley and I thought we would
have some unusual fun, so we disguised ourselves as beggars
and then put on old calico sunbonnets and with a letter stating
we were "two deserving women footing it, to join our brother
at Chattanooga," proceeded first to Mr. Frank Jones, our
nearest neighbor, where all went well, until a rain storm
forced us to reveal ourselves in order to get home. Their
astonishment was as great as our enjoyment was. When it
held up Mr. Jones sent us home on an old horse. I don't
think our home folks liked it much.

November 10th—

Our neighbor, Mr. Jones, was over to tell father that the
Federal Government had made a proposition for a six
months' armistice, during which time they will try and restore
the union, and if this is impossible, will let the South go in
peace.

November 23rd—

Next Tuesday night Mr. Freeman Goode, our merry old
neighbor and a grass widower, will give a large party. The
young people rely upon him for all their fun these war times.
Well the only beaux who will be there are those who are not
in the army, and were I a young lady I would not want their
attentions.

December 1st—

The girls gave a "candy stew" Friday night to Col. Fred
Ashford of the 16th Alabama Regiment. A number of
young ladies were present, but because of the war in our
midst very few men. (The 16th Alabama Regiment was
organized at Courtland, August 8, 1861.)

December 10th—

Here is such a lovely war poem I think it best to copy it
in my journal, since it is such a gem. (Here follows, "All
Quiet Along the Potomac To-night.")

### December 18th—

Last Monday Miss Kate Armistead, Captain McFarland of Florence, and Mr. Willie Irvine were at Mr. Goode's, where we and others were invited to dinner. There we unexpectedly stayed afterward to a dance, and several of the 1st Kentucky were there also.

### December 19th—

My brother, Dr. Saunders, has come from Chattanooga, quite weak from a spell of camp fever. Smallpox is also raging in both armies. Brother Robert also arrived from Tennessee.

### January 11th, 1863—

Dr. Saunders, wife and child, and Mary Wheatley, left on the 8th for Chattanooga, he to return to his post after illness. A great battle was fought at Murfreesboro: Heavy losses on both sides. Confederates as usual victorious.

### January 14th—

Last night a wounded soldier from the Murfreesboro battle asked to be permitted to spend the night. Of course we were only too glad to help one so brave and yet so unfortunate. He is afoot, so today father has sent him home in our carriage with a bed in it.

### January 24th—

My dearest friend, Loulie Redus of Mobile, writes that she—is at Mrs. Saunders' Female Academy, Tuscaloosa, Ala., where I hope soon to be also. She writes that the Military Cadets of Tuscaloosa are a glorious lot of boys.

### February 11th—

On the 3rd Lieutenant Sullivan, a nephew of Gen. Earl Van Dorn (and of his staff) spent the night here, en route to Tuscumbia, expecting to meet the General there, but upon finding he had not yet arrived he returned and has been with us several days. He is very well read, always like bright people. General Van Dorn will join General Bragg before

Murfreesboro, where they will fight Rosecrans. A battle at Fort Donelson a few days since, 200 negroes and much commissary captured.

### February 13th—

Lieutenant Sullivan went to Florence yesterday and tomorrow Van Dorn's troops will pass, going on to Shelby ville, Tenn., to join Bragg and to attack Rosecrans. General Roddy's corps has left Tuscumbia and also gone to join Bragg.

### February 23rd—

What a day of excitement. Father heard this morning that the Yankee gunboats had passed Tuscumbia where a short skirmish occurred, and are at Florence and the enemy may be hourly expected at Courtland. How horrible! My dear father, though very weak from his wound, will leave us and again rejoin the army; God protect his patriotic heart! O, the moon shines so bright and calm to-night, as if in mockery of our woes!

### March 1st—

I am writing with a light heart. The Yankees came up as far as Town Creek (four miles off), but since our men had destroyed all bridges and the water is high they could not ford the creek and they retired. They are destroying and burning property and compelling the people to pay war tax, and insulting ladies by searching them and even running their hands into their pockets! Father returned last night and General Bragg will send troops to defend the valley. Father went after them among the 16th Alabama and 37th Mississippi.

### March 4th—

The 16th Alabama is quartered at Huntsville.

### March 11th—

Yesterday I read General Van Dorn's reply to the charges made against him by Brig. Gen. John Bowers, and I think with President Davis it is the clearest defense I ever read. I pray this horrible war will soon be over and all the Yankees in "Davy Jones' locker." I continue a "notorious rebel." There is some talk of the Western states forming a part of our Confederacy. I say "die first."

### March 27th—

Yesterday Lieutenant Madding, Lieutenant Davis and Dr. Ed Ashford spent the morning here. Cousin Joe Parris and Captain Montgomery, of General Earl Van Dorn's staff, were here to dinner with us. Captain Grant, of Forrest's Brigade, is here for a few days. A year ago while riding my pony, Monti, I threw a bouquet to a soldier who was passing in the ranks, and now Captain Grant surprises me by saying that he was the soldier.

### March 29th—

I am trying to keep up my studies and daily horseback rides as well as the course of reading I have mapped out.

### April 8th—

Colonel Hannon of Montgomery, and Lieutenant Moncrief spent last night here and eight soldiers, four of whom were badly wounded.

When in January, 1861, two companies of soldiers were passing our big gate, I was there with a beautiful little Confederate flag in my hand, and officers and privates both begged for it, but with a little impromptu speech I gave it to a nice private, and he made me a beautiful response. A member of his company told me last night that he pinned that flag to his horse's head in the battle of Shiloh and hurrahed for me in the charge, and his name is Lieut. John Smith.

### April 11th—

This morning, one year ago, I saw the Federal soldiers surround the beautiful home for the first time, and insolently ask for my father, seventy-nine of them. So many to capture just one man. We have had so much trouble since then. But avant such unpleasant reminiscences.

April 19th—

General Roddy was ordered a week ago to Tuscumbia and on the 17th the Yankees advanced from Corinth to Big Bear Creek. Their force not known, but variously estimated from 15,000 to 20,000, while General Roddy has only 1,200 men. He captured a cannon. It is the general opinion that the Federals will immediately enter our valley, since our force is not strong enough to prevent. Captain Sloss's company was in the fight.

April 26th—

And I am in Huntsville, and a refugee. How strange! My sisters and Lawrie and I came here on the 22nd when the Yankees were within five miles of our home. Father will take Mother and Lizzie to a safe place also. We are with our aunt, Mrs. S. W. Harris.

May 2d—

We see much company, but sister says mother would not approve of my having beaux, so I do not have as nice a time as I might otherwise. I hear the Federal soldiers have reached Courtland and have burnt our house (a mistake). Lawrie has gone to Decatur to meet mother and bring her and the servants to Huntsville.

May 7th—

Mother and father went to Athens with servants and as the Federal soldiers are now back in Corinth they have returned home.

May 14th—

General Forrest arrived yesterday and also my father. They are going to visit General Bragg on military affairs.

May 15th—

While walking out on the pike last evening I threw some roses to General Forrest as he drove by us, and my glove went (unintentionally on my part) with them. He laughed and stopped to ask me if I "had challenged him"? "No,

indeed," I cried, "I would rather appoint so brave a man my
champion." Whereupon he thanked me quite gallantly.
Lieut. Wm. Forrest was with him.

### May 15th—

General and Mrs. Forrest will be given a reception at
Mrs. Robinson's to-night, and to-morrow the citizens will give
a reception and present General Forrest with an elegant war
steed.

### May 25th—

Rocky Hill!   Home again!   We travelled as far as
Decatur on the 18th with General Forrest and his staff.   Our
barouche met us there.   Gen. Bill Johnson is camped near us
and wrote a note last night asking that some supper be sent
him as he "was too tired and soiled to come for it," and this
morning he and his staff rode over to breakfast.   He was
accompanied by a guard of 200 men and his flag floated
proudly in the breeze.   They spent the morning with us,
until the stern laws of military forced their departure.   I
have never talked to so many officers at one time before.

### June 14th—

Our struggle for independence is hourly becoming more
bloody.   The sad, sad news has reached us that General
Forrest, our hero, Noble Forrest, is wounded.   How gladly
would I substitute myself rather than the South should lose
so able and chivalrous a defender.   When peace comes, how
happy would I feel could I exclaim, "My country, I, too, have
helped to win for you your glorious independence."   I try
to do all I can for our soldiers, but what is that compared
with what they suffer.   Were I a man I could fight for the
South, but I could not love her more.   But I am throwing
a shadow across your page, dear journal.

### July 26th—

It is thought this is the darkest hour of the Confederacy,
but still I hope.   It makes me angry to think the Yankees
can drive me from my home.   My sisters and I will go to

Columbus, Miss., and I from there to the Alabama Female College at Tuscaloosa. There is also a military college there, now, with 250 cadets. The Yankees are expected here in a few days, and Lawrie leaves Wednesday for the army. Capt. Will Forrest, brother of the general has been with us for sometime past, and is recovering from a wound in the leg.

#### August 21st—

A proclamation by President Davis making this a day of humiliation, fasting and prayer. Ah, how many prayers are wafted to the Throne of Light this day for fathers, husbands, brothers, sons and lovers. May God on high hear us! Captain Forrest is at Bailey Springs. He was thrown from his buggy and his wounded leg broken.

#### August 22d—

Would you know why I am so sad, my dear journal? Alas, a dear soldier friend of mine is dead (Fred A. Ashford, Colonel of the 16th Alabama). He fell nobly on the Altar of Liberty. Ah, we will think of you when our soldiers return with happy tramp from the war. I shall think of you when so gallantly rallying your men to the charge, though wounded, you cried, "Forward, my brave boys"! Your last words, I wonder if you know how desolate the death missle has made the hearts that love you.

#### August 25th—

The Tories (Jayhawkers) in the mountains between here and Tuscumbia, have organized into a band of marauders and rob all who travel that route. This makes me very uneasy as to my trip to Tuscaloosa.

#### September 16th—

A considerable change in military affairs since I last wrote. General Wheeler has ordered General Roddy to Gadsden and now our valley is left again exposed to the invader. Roddy is yet in the valley and our house has been headquarters for him and many agreeable officers, as they came and went. Lawrie leaves to-morrow with General Roddy's escort, my heart is sad, but that is his place, and there he should be.

September 19th—

Lawrie left with General Roddy. He will ultimately join General Forrest's command. Bragg has had a great battle with Rosecrans (Chickamauga). We were victorious. Great losses on both sides. The noble General Helm was killed, one of Kentucky's bravest sons. Oh, how we mourn him. He was here with us, and we know him well.

October 4th—

I thought I would have been at school in Tuscaloosa ere this, but the deserters and tories are still banded together in the mountains and intercept all travellers. So father fears to let me go.

October 10th—

General Wheeler and troops are in the valley, also General Stephen D. Lee of Mississippi, and General Wharton of Texas, General Wheeler sent a courier to father last night, saying that he and staff would be here, they crossed the river yesterday and the Yankees are just on the other side. Another courier has come and father has gone to meet the generals.

October 11th—

Well, last night came General Wheeler and staff, and Gen. Stephen D. Lee, and Gen. Sam Ferguson. All three are young to be generals. General Wheeler left for Decatur. His staff is composed of elegant gentlemen; Major Burford, Lieutenant Wailes, Major Pointer, and others. Major Pointer gave me a "five shooter," and Captain Nichols a beautiful crimson army sash, captured on the McMinnville raid in Tennessee, and General Wheeler displayed for our benefit the Federal flag he had captured there. General Wheeler returns to-morrow night.

### October 17th—

There was a concert in Courtland last night for the benefit of the 35th Alabama. All of us took a part. Sister Prue went with Captain Wade and I with Lieutenant Pointer, and I played "Whispering Winds" and "Wheeler's Polka," and was dressed in the Confederate colors.

### October 18th—

Lawrie arrived last night bringing dispatches from General Roddy to General Wheeler. He is pleased with "soldiering." Our house is crowded all the time.

### October 20th—

A large concert in town last night, and another to-night. Brass buttons have been very attractive of late.

### October 25th—

Alas, what a change has "come over the spirit of our dreams." All the military are gone. Generals Lee and Ferguson to meet the enemy below Tuscumbia, who are advancing in large force, General Wheeler to Guntersville. The Yankees, 2,500 strong, are as near as Mount Hope (this county), and we are also pent in on all sides and could not retreat if we would. They are tearing up every inch of railway between here and Decatur, and from present appearances the Yankees will be on us before the end of the week.

We have heard cannonading distinctly all day, and while I write the rapid booming of artillery shakes the house. General Lee, I suppose, is engaging the enemy. Ah, every report of those cannon hurries souls into the next world. It is terrible.

### April 9th—1864—

Tuscaloosa Female College— I cannot do without my journal. It is an intimate and living friend who never betrays. I am here alone, going to school, and my family are now scattered to the four winds. Some within Federal and some within Confederate lines, and others crossing the foaming ocean. And still "the baying of the dismal dogs of war answer, each other."

### April 23rd—

How lonely I feel at the end of the week. General Lee and General Ferguson are in town and came to see me on Wednesday.

### May 1st—

Tuscaloosa is filled with soldiers and many Missourians are among the numbers. I have just seen General French, Gen. Ed Johnson, Gen. George A. Johnston, Adjt. Gen. McCan, Capt. James Scanlan and Capt. Ed Terger. Friday there was a review of the Missouri troops. They are noble looking men, and Gen. S. D. Lee, General Jackson, General French and General Hodge with their staffs were present.

### May 2d—

Yesterday, Jennie and I were walking in front of the college and met General Jackson (Wm. H.) who jumped down from his horse and began talking to me, when his horse ran off. He ran after it and then returning, walked on with us, when I told him I "had just accomplished more than ever a Yankee had, for I had unhorsed him." His manner is very courtly. Friday night Jennie Mellon and I went to a large party given to General Lee, and he kindly sent to know if I would go with him, but Mrs. Saunders preferred not. We were also invited to Mrs. Figet's Saturday night, but did not accept.

"Free is his heart who for his country fights,
 He on the eve of battle may resign
  Himself to social pleasures; sweetest then
   When danger to the soldier's soul endears,
 The human joy that never may return.
            Douglas.

After the War—

My father and Lawrie were captured 11th of August, 1864. Father returned August 16th, but Lawrie was sent on to Nashville, and later to Camp Chase, O., where he languished until the surrender, coming home to die of illness contracted in prison.

Note:

It is related of the Little Rebel whose journal is given above that when she was only some fourteen years of age, Federal troops were encamped near her home, Rocky Hill, and the commander of the troops, out of respect for her father, Col. Jas. E. Saunders, placed a guard with Captain in charge to protect the home. The Captain was given his meals in the dining room, and was especially respectful and courteous. On leaving, he was taking his adieus on the porch, and extended his hand to Miss Ellen. She drew back, folded her hands behind her, and repeated these lines of the Douglas to Marmion:

"The hand of Douglas is his own,
And never shall in friendly grasp,
The hand of such as Marmion clasp."

To which the Captain raised his hat and laughingly departed.

MACFARLANE CLAN ARMORIAL BEARING.

# McFARLAND FAMILY.

The McFarlands came from the Highlands of Scotland. Their name was spelled Mac-farlane in Scotland, but more than one branch that came to America changed the spelling to McFarland.

The earliest record we find of the clan was of Malcom, the Sixth Laird, who obtained a charter of the lands in 1395, on the Western shore of Loch Lomond. In 1493, Andrew Mac-farlane, by marriage with a daughter of the Earl of Lennox, succeeded in reclaiming the lands held by the clan. Sir John Mac-farlane was knighted by the King the night before the battle of Flodden, and was slain in battle next day.

Hollingshead, speaking of the battle of Langside, says: "A Highland gentleman named Mac-farlane, saved the battle for the Regents by his valor against the Queen's forces." Sir Walter Scott writes of the clan as "The wild Mac-farlane, plaided clan."

In 1547, Walter Mac-farlane was among the slain at Pinkey.

In 1587, Andrew Mac-farlane was made responsible for the clan, as owner of their lands.

In 1644, the clan followed Montrose.

Mr. Skein, in his works on the Highland clans, speaks of one Walter Mac-farlane, celebrated among collectors and historians, who claimed for his clan's ancestors renown for their prowess in arms.

One branch of the clan removed to Ireland during the reign of James VII, and was represented by Mac-farlane of Huntstonhouse in Dublin County. Another branch came to America in the early part of the eighteenth century, and the home of the chief going to America became the property of the Duke of Argyle.

The clan's plaid is a red ground checked with white and black, the white bordering the black on either side.

The writer has a copy of the coat of arms of the clan, brought from Scotland by Mr. Graham McFarlane, of Clarksville, Tennessee, who had recently visited the McFarlane castle.

The Mac-farlanes and Grahams (originally spelled Graem, hero and lover of Ellen Douglass of the Lady of the Lake) were often in feud, while the Campbell clan was in alliance with Mac-farlane. The old Scotch song, "The Campbells are coming, Oh-ho, Oh-ho" had its origin from this: The Graems attacked the Mac-farlane castle, and were about to starve them to surrender. The Campbells came to their rescue, and as the Mac-farlanes awoke one morning, they saw the Campbell banner coming, and they raised the cry, "The Campbells are coming, Oh-ho, Oh-ho."

The writer's wife was a Graham. We were never in serious feud, but I sometimes jokingly call for the Campbells.

There were two branches of the clan that came from Scotland and their descendants settled in Tennessee, one descending from John, and the other from David McFarland. John settled in East Tennessee, and their descendants have included many useful and distinguished citizens, among them John McFarland, of Morristown, a colonel in the Confederate army; another, Robert McFarland, a brother, for many years Judge of the Supreme Court of Tennessee, greatly respected as a Judge, and beloved as a man, and from the female branches have also descended many honored names, among others, the Bradfords and Bartons, one, Judge Robert M. Barton, a distinguished Judge of the Court of Appeals of Tennessee, still living.

These two branches were undoubtedly from the same stem, having a general personal likeness, the same family given names, and acceptedly recognized as kin by the older members of the families.

*The branch from which the writer descended.*
*Daniel and Mary McFarland.*

Daniel McFarland was born March 9, 1746, in Caswell or Tazwell County, North Carolina, and moved from there to White County, Tennessee, where he died October 17, 1816. He married Mary Scott, b. March 20, 1746, d. Oct. 22, 1788. His second wife was Mary Boyd, by whom he had two children, David and Henderson. He served as Colonel in the Revolutionary War.

*Issue of Daniel McFarland and Mary Scott.*

   I.   Lewis—b. 5 July, 1774; d. 3 Feby. 1860.
   II.  Rebecca—b. 12 Feby. 1776; d. 17 Nov. 1779.
   III. Caleb—b. 6 Feby. 1782; d. 3 Feby. 1860.

   I. Lewis McFarland married Oct. 4, 1803, Ann Jamison, (b. Jany. 31, 1788; d. June 24, 1846) daughter of Thomas and Jane Jamison. They both came from North Carolina and settled near Dixon Springs, Smith County, Tennessee, near the Cumberland River. Upon this homestead Lewis lived until his death, and reared his family. He was fond of and bred fine horses; whence his sons and grandsons inherited their fondness for thoroughbred and standard horses.

*Issue of Lewis McFarland and Anne Jamison:*

   I.    Mary—b. 6 Dec., 1804; d. 4 Dec., 1854. Leaving no issue.
   II.   John—b. 1 Oct., 1806; d. 4 Feby., 1870.
   III.  Wilson Yandel—b. 24 July, 1809; d. 23 July, 1872.
   IV.   William Felix—b. 6 Sept., 1811; d. 3 Jany., 1878.
   V.    Henry—b. Nov., 1813; d. 7 Jany., 1835. No issue.
   VI.   Romulus—b. 16 May, 1816; d. 12 March, 1818. No issue.
   VII.  Eliza Jane—b. 18 July, 1818; d. 16 Mar., 1896. (Married John Elliott, no children.)
   VIII. James H.—b. 13 Jany., 1821; d. 9 Sept., 1822.

IX.    Martha Anna—b. 7 May, 1823; d. 17 July, 1846. No issue.

X.    George P.—b. 10 Nov., 1825; d. 6 Dec., 1881.

XI.    Susan C.—b. 12 June, 1828; d. 24 Feb., 1859.

II.    John McFarland—Married Harriett B. Shepherd, who died 20 June, 1854; and second wife, Adeline Scruggs; b. 2 Dec., 1831; d. 2 Oct., 1883.

*Issue of John and Harriett:*

1. Thomas Joiner—b. 10 Dec., 1843; d. 7 Jan., 1900. Married Medora Byars, b. 29, Mch., 1843; d. 10 Feb., 1894. They had one son, John, b. 7 Aug., 1871; d. 15 Sept., 1872.

2. Thomas Lewis—b. 14 Dec., 1840; d. 17 March, 1841.

3. William Felix—b. 20 Jan., 1842; d. 31 March, 1854.

4. Edward Stoughton—b. 28 Jany., 1843; d.

5. John Milton—b. 6 May, 1848; d. 12 Feby., 1902. Married Minnie Frost, 7 Dec., 1875.

*Issue of John Milton and Minnie:*

(1) Corrinne—b. 27 Sept., 1876; m. John K. Kay.
   *Issue Corrinne and John K. Kay:*
   (a) Elizabeth Stuart—b. 1 Oct., 1902.
   (b) Alice Frost—b. 1 Sept., 1906.

(2) Edward Frost—b. Oct. 7, 1878. (Now in Korea.)

(3) Beaulah—b. Jany. 20, 1885, and a son named John Milton, born in 1887, both died in infancy.

*Issue of John McFarland and Adeline Scruggs:*

6. Lewis Brantley—b. Aug. 27, 1857; d. Sept. 29, 1916. Married Tommis Smith, Feb. 24, 1857.

*Issue ·*

(1) Eliza—b. Dec. 24, 1887.
(2) Ella Clyde—b. Jan. 5, 1890.
(3) Clara—b. Oct. 4, 1898.

7. Ida—b. July 27, 1860; d. Oct. 8, 1883.
8. Beaulah—b. Jany. 1, 1863; d. Sept. 15, 1883.
9. Sallie—b. July 7, 1865; d. Oct. 10, 1867
10. Lilly—b. Oct. 24, 1867; d. Aug., 1870.

III. *Wilson Yandell McFarland*—b. Feb. 28, 1809; d. Feb. 21, 1872. Married Oct. 15, 1853, Mary E. Sum mers; b. Dec. 15, 1818; d. May 21, 1861

He studied law under Judge Joe Guild, Gallatin, Tenn., and was licensed to practice in 1836, but wishing to join the patriots of Texas he went there, but peace being declared shortly he settled at Washington, where he practiced law for some years. Then moved to Belton and soon took prominence there and was unanimously elected Judge of that 'Judicial District and served for years until displaced by a Military Governor when he resumed his practice. He was regarded as one of the foremost lawyers and citizens and highly esteemed until his death.

*Issue of Wilson Yandell McFarland and Mary E. Summers:*

1. Emily Gill—b. Nov. 13, 1854; m. Dec. 23, 1870, Frederick H. Austin, b. Nov. 26, 1844; d. Oct. 30, 1910. Had only one child, Mabel A., b. July 11, 1876; d. March 5, 1905.

2. Anna Lewis—b. Feb. 8, 1856; m. 28 Oct., 1880, William Francis Adger Ellison, b. 1853.

*Issue:*

(1) Wilson, McF. E.—b. July 18; m. Sept. 15, 1907; Louisa Cook, b. Aug. 24, 1883.

*Issue:*

Henry Austin—b. 27 June, 1908.
Wilson McF., Jr.—b. 27 Aug., 1912.
Howard—b. 28 Feby., 1918.

(2) Alfred E.—b. 5 Nov. 1887; m. 9 June, 1917.

*Issue:*

a. Alfred J.—b.

(3) Peyton, Austin E.—b. 25 June, 1893.

3. James Davis McFarland—b. 14 Oct., 1885; d. 16 May, 1885.

4. Mary Summers McFarland—b. 14 Feby., 1860, m. Dec. 15, 1872, Charles William Peyton.

IV *William Felix McFarland:*—b. Sept. 6, 1811; m. June 28, 1842, Martha Ann Douglass, daughter of Burchette Douglass and Martha McGee (see Douglass).

*Issue of William Felix and Martha Ann:*

1. Louis Burchette—b. April 7, 1843; m. April 4, 1872, Ellen Virginia Saunders, b. Dec. 18, 1848; d. June 30, 1900; m. (2nd wife) Floy Graham Allen, daughter of Barnet Graham and wife. Married at Sewanee, Tennessee, by Bishop Thos. F. Gailor.

2. Emma Caroline—b. March 17, 1845; d. June 2, 1846.

3. Anna Elizabeth—b. Feb. 24, 1847; d. April 11, 1885; m. D. M. Neblett.

*Issue ·*

(1) L. M. Neblett—b.          ; m. 28 Sept., 1898, Laura Graves; Sept. 28, 1893.

*Issue:*

(a) Laura Elizabeth—b. 19 Sept., 1899.
(b) Ellen McFarland—b. 5 March, 1901.

(2) Ellen V.—b. 19 Feby., 1881; m. C. H. Woodyard, 21 Oct., 1903; b. 15 Oct., 1872, Ft. Worth, Texas.

*Issue:*

(a) Lewin N.—b. 12 Feby., 1906.

(b) James Douglass—b. 27 April, 1907.

(c) Charles S.—b. 27 June, 1915.

4. Ella Medora—b. Feby. 15, 1849; d. June 20, 1857.

5. Henry Wilson—b. Aug. 29, 1851; d. Aug. 2, 1852.

6. Felix Addison—b. May 7, 1855; m. Strayhorn, b. ; d. 5 October, 1921.

*Issue:*

(1) Lula Maud—b. ; m. Nicholson.

*Issue:*

(a) Lamar—b. April 23, 1907.

(b) Wilson—b. Jany., 1911.

(c) Louis—b. 1914.

Felix Addison's second wife, Laura Stuart, m.

*Issue ·*

(1) Felix Stuart—b. April 5, 1900.

(2) Burchette Douglass—b. March 12, 1902.

(3) Floy K.—b. Sept. 8, 1906.

(4) Martha Nell—b. Oct. 28, 1908.

7. Henry Douglass—b. Jany., 1857; d. Oct., 1857.

8. John Rush—b. 1858; d. Dec. 1863.

9. Lillian—b. 1860; d. Dec. , 1863.

10. Henry—b. 1862; d. Dec. , 1863.

X. George P. McFarland, M. D.—b. 10 November, 1825; d. 6th Dec., 1881; m. 30th Sept., 1855, Mary L. Alexander, b. 1st July, 1836; d. 6th May, 1911.

*Issue*:

1. William L.—b. 21 July 1856; m. 7 Sept., 1882, Ida S. Freeman.

2. Adam Wilson—b. 19th, September, 1858; d. July, 1885.

3. George P., Jr.—b. 9 Jan., 1861; d. 16 Nov., 1904.

4. John Lee—b. 16 Nov., 1869; d.          m.

5. Anna Elizabeth—b. 29 Aug., 1873; d. 22 Dec., 1904; m. J. H. Gullege, 26 June, 1902; d.

   *Issue*:
   Stephen Hampton Gullege—b. May, 1903.

6. Mary Eliza—b. 29 Nov., 1875; d. 6 Oct., 1876.

7. Marion Burchette—b. Oct. 27th, 1879; d. 15 June, 1901.

XI. *Susan C. McFarland*—b. June 12, 1828; d. Feb. 24, 1859; m. F. L. Davidson.

*Issue*·

1. Geo. L. Davidson—b. Feb. 19, 1856; m. Nov. 30, 1892, Kate E. Eddins.

   *Issue*
   (1) Ruth Eliza—b. June 22, 1894.

   (2) Katherine Eddins—b. March 18, 1898; m. James          Knight, Jr., 1921.

MRS. MARTHA DOUGLASS.

HON. BURCHETT DOUGLASS.

# LINEAGE OF THE DOUGLASS FAMILY.

Edward Douglass, who came to America from Scotland, married Sarah George, in Fauquier County, Virginia, in 1740.

In the fall of 1785, he, with his family moved to Sumner County, Tennessee, their children are as follows:

John Douglass—(Killed by Cherokee Indians).

William Douglass—Married Peggy Strand, Orange Co. N. C.

Elizabeth Douglass—Married Wm. Cage of Virginia.

Elmore Douglass—Married Elizabeth Blakemore of Sumner County, Tennessee.

Ezekial Douglass—Married Polly Gibson of Sumner Co. Tennessee.

Sally Douglass—Married Thos. Blakemore, of Sumner County, Tennessee.

Edward Douglass—Married Elizabeth Howard of Chatham, N. C.

Reuben Douglass—Married Elizabeth Edwards of Sumner County, Tennessee.

James Douglass—Married Catherine Collier, Raleigh, N. C.

---

Elmore Douglass—Born, January 16th, 1753.

Elizabeth Blakemore Douglass—Born, February 8th, 1761 (Wife), their children are as follows:

John Douglass—Born November 13th, 1777; d. 3 July, 1807.

Celia Douglass Page—Born December 4th, 1779; d. 9 Sept. 1844.

Sarah Douglass Hooks—Born February 21st, 1782.

Nancy Douglass Payston—Born March 26th, 1784.

Elizabeth Douglass Cooper—Born January 13th, 1786; d. 1 Apl. 1816.

Burchett Douglass—Born October 6th, 1793.; d. 31 July, 1849.

Ennis Douglass—Born February 13th, 1796.

Elmore Douglass—Born March 4th, 1798.

Ila Douglass—Born November 17th, 1799.

Delia Douglass Brook—Born February 1st, 1801.

Asa B. Douglass—Born February 10th, 1803

Burchett Douglass, sixth son of Elmore and Elizabeth Blakemore Douglass, was born 6th October, 1793, and died 31st, July, 1849. Married 23d, Feb. 1819, Martha McGee, one of the McGee family of Middle Tennessee, famous in the Methodist ministry of Tennessee. She died at the old homestead Fayette County, Tenn., 23d, September, 1874.

Burchett Douglass was born in Wilson County, Tenn., lived there for many years and represented that county in the State Senate from early manhood to his removal from the county to Fayette County, Tenn., and also as member of the Constitutional Convention, 1834.

He moved to Somerville, Fayette County, where he established a bank of which he was president until his death.

He also owned a large plantation on Muddy Creek, in northern portion of the county which remained the family home for many years.

He was a prominent whig in politics, and when he moved to Fayette that county had for many years gone Democratic by a large majority, and it became difficult to get a whig candidate for the State House or Senate.

His popularity and prestige in debate suggested him as a champion Whig, and he was finally persuaded to contest for the Senate, against the Democratic candidate, then member of Senate, and boasted invincible.

They made an active and notable canvass, and Mr. Douglass was elected by a large majority. The older citizens of that county delighted to tell the writer of his grandfather's eloquent and persuasive speeches, his popularity and his great virtues as a citizen.

He was also a soldier under Gen. Jackson, and fought under him in the Indian battles Emagfan—Talladega and others.

He was buried at Dancyville near his home, and his epitaph reads as follows: "He was an active member of the Convention which framed the present Constitution. Was twenty-five years in public life without a defeat. His public worth lives in the archives of his state, his private virtues in the lives of his children."

*Issue Burchett Douglass and Martha McGee.*

I. Adison Hamilton Douglass.

Born in Somerville, Tennessee, 28th, Aug. 1824, and soon after graduating he settled in Memphis, Tenn., and lived there until his death which occurred, 3rd, Sept. 1894.

He soon became one of its prominent citizens, first alderman for a number of years, then mayor of the city. He was the whig candidate for Congress against Knox Walker, the Democratic candidate, and they made a brilliant canvass over the district, but Democracy prevailed.

He was afterwards elected Judge of the Criminal Court and served some years in that office.

His first wife was Martha Robinson, who died 11th, Sept. 1848, leaving one daughter, Elizabeth Anna, born 2nd, Aug. 1845, and died in youth.

He married, 24th April, 1859, his second wife, Elizabeth Bullock Randolph, of Macon, Ga., b. 24th, April, 1850, d. 30th, April, 1886.

*Issue of Addison H. and Elizabeth R. Douglass:*

1. Richard Randolph Douglas—b. Feb. 7, 1856; m. 7 Sept., 1892, Minnie J. Baily, b. 7 Sept., 1892; d. 27 March, 1912. He married his second wife, Edith L. Collier, 6 July, 1916.

*Issue:*

(1) Richard R. Douglas, Jr.—b. 18 April, 1896; m.

> *Issue:*
>
> (a) Richard Randolph, III—b. 23 Jan., 1922.

2. Ida May Douglas—b. 5 May, 1857; m. 22 Nov., 1882, Edwin F. Wills, b. 11 Jan., 1850; d. 14 Aug., 1919.

   *Issue:*

   (1) Ida May Wills—b. 15 Nov., 1886; m. 28 Jan., 1908, Rev. John Meyers.

   > *Issue·*
   >
   > (a) Ida Lucille Meyers—b. 30 March, 1909.
   >
   > (b) Elizabeth Meyers—b. 19 Sept., 1910.
   >
   > (c) Edith Meyers—b. 21 Jan, 1912.

   (2) Walter D. Wills—b. 25 Jan., 1886; m. Caroline Duval.

   (3) Addie Randolph Wills—b. 18 Mar., 189 ; m. Apr. 23, 1918, Wm. R. Archibald.

3. Addie H. Douglass—b. 7 Dec., 1860; m. 21 June, 1893, Herbert S. Shepherd, b. 8 Jan., 1856.

   *Issue:*

   (1) Douglass Newton Shepherd—b. 23 Aug., 1894.

   (2) Herbert Randolph Shepherd—b. 11 June, 1896.

   (3) Charles Francis Shepherd—b. 19 April, 1898.

4. Mattie Douglass—b. 24 Dec., 1865; m. 21 Oct., Will Stewart Parks, b. 20 March, 1861.

   *Issue:*

(1) Martha Manier Parks—b. 31 Aug.. 1897.

(2) Will Douglass Parks—b. 31 Oct., 1898.

(3) Anna Shepherd Parks—b. 20 March, 1901.

(4) Ellen Randolph Parks—b. 11 March, 1904.

5. Eugene Burchett Douglass—b. 14 Oct., 1886; m. 28 Aug.. 1896, Alice Mallory, b. 6 Dec., 18 8.

*Issue:*

(1) Eugene Burchett Douglass, Jr.—b. 7 May, 1891. Volunteered in. the Great War. Joined the 281 Aero Squadron, in France. Served gallantly and died September, 19..., at St. Mafaient,. France. Now sleeps in Elmwood Cemetery, Memphis.

(2) Lucille Alice Douglass—b. 20 Oct., 1891; m.

II. Caroline McGee Douglass—b. 11 Jany., 1826; d. 3 July, 1865; m. 22 April, 1847, Solomon H. Shaw.

*Issue:*

1. Martha Emma Shaw—b. 24 April, 1849; d. 19 April, 1905, m. C. Curtis, 8 June, 1870.

*Issue:*

(1) May Curtis—b. 7 May, 1872; m. Dr. J. F Rawlings, 8 Dec., 1896; d..

*Issue*

(a) Melville Rawlings—b.

(2) Melville Shaw Curtis—b. 14 June, 1874.

III. Martha Ann Douglass—b. 9 Nov., 1823; d. 3 June. 1878; m. 28 June, 1842, Dr. W. F. McFarland. (See McFarland Family.)

IV. Henry L. Douglass—born 11 Jan., 1826; d. (No family record furnished.)

V.    John Elmore Douglass—b. 27 Oct., 1827; d. 10 April, 1909; m. 29 Feb., 1852, Sallie Pruett; d.       ; m. second wife, Mrs. Martha Phillips.

*Issue*:

1.   Willis Ballard Douglass—b. 15 July, 1874; m. 28 Nov., 1897, Martha Randle Peebles.

*Issue ·*

(1)   John Elmore Douglass—b. 25 Jan., 1904.

(2)   Benjamin Peebles Douglass—b. 24 Aug., 1910.

2.   Lena Douglass—b.      ; m.      Jeter.

VI.    W. B. Douglass—b. 17 March     ; d. 17 Dec.. 1881; m. Henrietta B. Hare, 14 January, 1857. (No issue.)

VII.    Elizabeth B. Douglass—b. 12 Oct., 1828; d. 21 Apr., 1864; m. John Beverly Robinson, b. 18 March, 1852; d. 8 Oct., 1888.

*Issue*:

1.   John Douglass Robinson—b. 18 March, 1852; d. 3 Sept., 1878; m. Anna Pickett.

*Issue*:

Douglass Robinson.

2.   William Henry Robinson—b. 18 Dec., 1856; d. 15 Nov., 1887.

3.   Leila Robinson—b.      ; m. 10 Dec., 1873, Alston Boyd—b. 25 Sept., 1850; d. 4 Nov., 1896.

*Issue*:

(1)   Elizabeth Boyd—b.      d. 8 Nov., 1907; m. Fontaine Wade,

*Issue*:

(a)   Alston Boyd Wade—b.      ; m. Fay Ogilbie, 6 Aug., 1918.

*Issue*:

Fay Ogilbie Wade—b. 16 Feb., 1920.

(b)   Leila Boyd Wade.

(2) Mary Boyd—b.          ; m. A. G. Wagner.

(3) Alston Boyd—b. Feb. 15, 1879; m. Julia
Wetter.

*Issue*:

Alston Boyd, Jr.—b. 3 March, 1913.

(4) Leila Boyd—b.

(5) Martha Boyd—b.

(6) Douglass Boyd—b.             ; d.

4.  John Beverly Robinson—b.

CPSIA information can be obtained
at www.ICGtesting.com
Printed in the USA
BVOW06s0858120517

483961BV00014B/211/P

9 781333 405830